# Overcoming L[...]

**Alice Muir** trained at the University c[...]
Jordanhill College in Glasgow and also wi[...]
Chartered Psychologist, qualified teacher of psychology, science and mathematics, an experienced trainer, author and Life Coach, and has a Diploma in Counselling and in Cognitive Behavioural Therapy. Alice has had a long-standing interest in both psychology and personal development, and has been lecturing, writing and training on these subjects – as well as coaching groups and individuals – for over 25 years. She helped to set up the Scottish charity 'Stresswatch Scotland' in 1982, and helping to secure its Government funding has been one of her most satisfying achievements. Alice was the first to use the term 'Stress Adviser' in 1994, and has trained hundreds of Stress Advisers all over the UK and overseas since then.

Currently an Associate Lecturer and Study Support Tutor with the Open University, Alice is a member of the British Psychological Society, the General Teaching Council, the Society of Authors, the Association for Coaching, and is a Fellow of the International Stress Management Association (ISMA UK). She is Features Editor on ISMA's journal *Stress News* (where she has had a regular *'Web is the Word'* column since 2004), and has provided 'expert comments' for many articles, including those in *My Weekly, Psychologies, Prima, Mail on Sunday, The Herald* and *Essentials* magazine. Alice has written seven books, including *Coping with a Stressed Nervous System* and *Make Your Sensitivity Work for You* (Sheldon Press), and *Teach Yourself Relaxation, Blissful Relaxation,* and – in conjunction with ITV's 'This Morning' – *Overcome Your Postnatal Depression* (Hodder Arnold).

# Overcoming Common Problems Series

*Selected titles*

A full list of titles is available from Sheldon Press,
36 Causton Street, London SW1P 4ST and on our website at
www.sheldonpress.co.uk

Overcoming Common Problems

# Overcoming Loneliness

ALICE MUIR

First published in Great Britain in 2012

Sheldon Press
36 Causton Street
London SW1P 4ST
www.sheldonpress.co.uk

*British Library Cataloguing-in-Publication Data*
A catalogue record for this book is available from the British Library

ISBN 978-1-84709-160-4
eBook ISBN 978-1-84709-231-1

Typeset by Fakenham Prepress Solutions, Fakenham, Norfolk NR21 8NN
Printed in Great Britain by Ashford Colour Press
Subsequently digitally printed in Great Britain

Produced on paper from sustainable forests

# Contents

# Introduction

Most people, asked to define loneliness, might talk about how it feels to be on your own for long periods. Or they might mention older people living by themselves, or having no friends, and how this can make you feel cut off from the world. Loneliness is about all of these. But it is also about much more.

You can also feel alone in an unhappy marriage, or among a group of friends or colleagues you just can't relate to, or in a room brimming with chattering people. Because loneliness isn't always about not having friends or not having people around you. It's about how you feel inside. It's about feeling isolated in some way, or totally alone with an experience you've had, or with a problem or situation you are facing. So you can feel terribly lonely if you're being bullied or victimized, or if you have something difficult to cope with, such as a cancer diagnosis, a marriage break-up, a failed venture or a bereavement. No matter how active you are and how many friends you have, almost nothing feels more lonely than having a personal sadness or a troubling worry. Or there can be that aching loneliness if someone you love is no longer with you, for whatever reason. Missing that person and his or her contribution to your life can be a feeling which seldom leaves you.

I also know many people who, despite leading a relatively trouble-free life with a good circle of friends and an active social life, still feel lonely because they are sure that they have so much less going on in their lives than other people. We tend to compare ourselves with others, and with today's world appearing to be full of happy, busy people, with lots of friends, all socializing and enjoying themselves, it's easy to feel we don't have as much of that as we should have. But this impression of the world is just one aspect of it, reflected many times through the bright magnifying lens of television, advertising, newspapers and all the rest. In the real world, most people lead relatively quiet and hard-working lives, without endless socializing and activity. And if living alone, as many people are, caring for a loved one or small children, or unemployed, they may speak to few people each day, if anyone.

Whatever your reason for reading this and your interest in loneliness, I hope this book will be your guide and support. I hope it will provide you with suggestions on how to feel less alone, no matter how that has come about. As this book will show, loneliness is a natural feeling, and the pain is real. 'The most terrible poverty is loneliness and the feeling of being unloved,' said Mother Teresa of Calcutta. The good news is that there is plenty you can do about it. So, breaking out of that 'poverty' is going to be life-changing and something you owe to yourself to do. Loneliness can be felt in your head and deep in your heart and soul, and it is in these places that I hope this book will help you to find ways to overcome your loneliness.

# 1

# Questions about loneliness

Newspaper and magazine articles or TV documentaries about loneliness typically feature a picture of a person sitting alone, looking sadly out of a window or staring blankly into the fire. Most of us at some point in our lives have experienced the empty feeling of being entirely on our own and cut off from the world. I can well remember feeling like that, as far back as my first day at school, when I knew absolutely no-one in a class brimming with around 35 other lively five year olds. Many of us can remember the fleeting pang of isolation we felt if we were last to be picked when two teams were being chosen for games at school. Or later in life, alone in your flat, hearing the happy chatter of neighbours, or finding yourself sitting on your own for lunch at work or at college.

> Amanda, the daughter of an old friend of mine, had been lucky enough to land the job she'd always dreamed of, as a graphic artist with an important company. Amanda was thrilled, and her family and friends were delighted for her. The job was in a town about 200 miles away from her home, but this didn't matter. Just turned 29 and single, Amanda enthusiastically flat-hunted and moved to the new town, full of energy and ambition for the future. But just recently my friend called me, as she was worried about Amanda. She had been phoning home in tears almost every other day, saying that she had no friends, didn't know the area and was just sitting in her flat night after night, and even at weekends, feeling isolated and lonely. Things were so bad, she was even thinking of giving up her job and coming home.

Loneliness like this does make people just want to give up and return to the security of family and friends, but there is so much Amanda can do to make things better, so that she doesn't have to give up her dream job. There is so much anyone who is lonely, whatever the reason, can do to make life feel better, and that's what this book is all about.

But how Amanda was feeling isn't the only type of loneliness. There are other kinds of loneliness, as George's story will show.

> On a very bright August day, several years ago, I met George, quite by chance, at a large local flower show. He was standing alone in one of the huge show tents, admiring the rows and rows of beautiful roses. As soon as I approached, he nodded a 'Good morning' and said, 'Aren't they wonderful?' Although complete strangers, we were soon in conversation about roses, gardening and putting the world to rights. He had persuaded his son, who had come with him to the flower show, to take a walk outside for some fresh air. George, as he introduced himself to me, had been growing roses for 20 years, but had never been confident enough to enter a show like this. He just enjoyed coming to admire the displays. He told me that Ella, his wife of 25 years, had died suddenly three years previously, and she had just adored roses. He chewed his lip and tears were close as he told me how good his family and friends had been to him when she died, and still were. He always had at least one visitor every day, and his son and daughter took him out as often as they could. But whenever his front door closed and he was on his own again, the house was so quiet and so empty without his wife. The day stretched ahead, and he felt so alone he almost couldn't bear it, even now, three years later. George has a good family and many loyal friends, and he gets out and about socially. But he still experiences loneliness.

What George is going through seems quite different from how Amanda is feeling. The positions they find themselves in are a lifetime apart too. Despite the similarities on the surface, these would appear to be two different types of loneliness, which are quite unlike each other.

## What is loneliness?

Loneliness hurts. It hurts a lot. It's not an actual physical pain, but it can feel like it, with an aching sensation deep inside your heart, your stomach or your entire body. You may feel trapped, with a longing for things to feel normal again. The good news is there are ways to overcome those painful feelings. That's why I have written this book.

It's clear that loneliness has many different aspects, and we all have our own ideas about what it means to us. It's also important to draw a line between people who simply enjoy their own company, and may need more solitude than others, and those for whom being alone, even for short periods, is an unhappy experience.

Loneliness is more common than you might expect. The Campaign to End Loneliness was launched in the UK in 2011. It was supported by a number of key organizations working together: these were Independent Age, Counsel and Care, Age UK Oxfordshire and the WRVS. A report produced by the campaign puts it very well: 'Loneliness is an emotional response to a perceived gap between the amount of personal contact an individual wants and the amount they have.'

## Two types of loneliness

George and Amanda were both lonely, and this idea of loneliness being the outcome of a gap between the social contact you have and the social contact you would like to have is true for them both too. But their experiences were still different from each other. Professor Vanessa Burholt, a sociologist, provides an explanation when she talks of two types of loneliness: social and emotional. She explains that *emotional loneliness* is the absence of a close bond and attachment to a partner or best friend, whereas *social loneliness* is felt if you lack a broad group of friends, neighbours and colleagues.

Social loneliness is probably the type most people associate with being lonely: feeling alone because of a lack of contact with friends, neighbours or the outside world in general – in other words, the lack of a social network.

Emotional loneliness can be experienced in a room full of people and even if you have a fantastic social network. This is because you don't have a special person to share emotional intimacy with. Emotional loneliness comes about because a close intimate attachment with a friend or partner has been lost, or has never existed. This leaves an empty space in an otherwise full life, and you carry it with you no matter where you are, even in a crowd of friends.

Emotional loneliness can also affect those who long for a child but remain childless, or parents separated from their children, or adults who have lost a parent; likewise for those who yearn for a grandchild or have been separated from their grandchildren. Table 1.1 shows just some of the typical effects these two types

**Table 1.1 What loneliness can feel like**

| Social loneliness | Emotional loneliness | Both |
|---|---|---|
| Bored | Desolate | Unhappy |
| Excluded | Empty | Anxious |
| Frustrated | Aching inside | Insecure |
| Low self-esteem | Heavy heart | Depressed |
| Worthless | Longing | Isolated |
| Ashamed | Yearning | Angry |
| Guilty | | Pessimistic |
| Useless | | Emotional 'pain' |
| Rejected | | Needing to belong |
| Longing to be part of | | Negative |
| a group | | Stressed |
| Unwanted | | Difficulty trusting people |
| | | Feeling trapped |
| | | Aimless |

of loneliness can have, though there is nothing hard and fast about which column an effect should appear in. There is plenty of crossover as loneliness is a highly individual experience.

## Nothing to be ashamed of

The Mental Health Foundation (MHF) suggests that though loneliness is very common, it can still be embarrassing to admit to it, because of associations of being unlikeable, unwanted or unworthy. But this just shouldn't be – feeling lonely is nothing to be ashamed of. It's a completely natural feeling and can happen to anyone, however strong or weak that person may be. Research confirms it is likely to happen to all of us at some point in our lives, and that lonely people are no less attractive or intelligent than their non-lonely counterparts. In fact, loneliness appears to have a social purpose and, according to the latest research, may even be programmed into us to ensure we stay with the group – much more on this in Chapter 4, which looks at the strong biological and psychological forces behind loneliness.

## Loneliness is widespread

Many people feel lonely today, whether old or young, men or women, rich or poor. From the young woman just embarked on a university course in a city far from home, to the lone parent coping with two small children, or the recently divorced 40-something year old, or even the lottery winner who doesn't know who her friends are any more. Even the rich and famous can be lonely, especially when they are out of the limelight. Robbie Williams, the English singer who became famous as part of the group Take That, wrote a song about loneliness when he went solo, called 'Singing for the Lonely'. Judy Garland, at the height of her fame as an American actress, said, 'It's lonely and cold at the top.' Janis Joplin, the American rock singer, famously said, 'On stage I make love to 25,000 people, and then I go home alone.' No matter who you are, the feeling of isolation and not having anyone to turn to or share your thoughts with is the same.

Despite the tendency to see loneliness as a problem confined mainly to older people, this is not so. The chances are that we will all experience loneliness at some point in our lives. Recent research in the UK has confirmed that feeling lonely is a major concern for one in every five of 18–24 year olds, compared with one in every ten of those aged 55 and over. In 2010, the MHF were so concerned that they produced a report on loneliness called *The Lonely Society?*, which concluded that one in ten of us 'often feel lonely'. This represents a huge number of people, over six million of us in the UK, many of them young people.

Small wonder, then, that this is often described as an 'epidemic of loneliness'.

## Can you measure loneliness?

For a very general way to measure loneliness, you can try the following activity. (Keep a notebook handy for the exercises and activities suggested through the book.)

1  Give each of these statements a score between 0 and 5 as to how true they are most of the time for you right now, 0 being 'not true at all' and 5 being 'true most of the time'. Don't think too

long about your answer, just think for a few moments and then answer:

(a)  I feel isolated from other people.
(b)  I have no-one to talk to.
(c)  I don't have a group of friends.
(d)  I miss having really close friends.
(e)  I miss having a sexual partner.
(f)  I miss having a partner to talk to.
(g)  No-one really knows me.
(h)  I miss having a best friend.
(i)  I feel lonely most of the time.
(j)  I'm not close to anyone.

2  Now add up your score, which will be out of a possible 50. A score of 0 will mean you're not currently lonely at all, and 50 that you are extremely lonely right now, with scores between 0 and 50 showing increasing levels of loneliness.

Another way of measuring loneliness was used by researchers in America in 1985. They asked a cross-section of people how many 'confidants' they had, and the most common answer was three. So that meant most people had three people they could confide in and talk openly with. The same procedure was repeated in 2004, and the most common reply, surprisingly, was none. One in four of those questioned said they had no-one they could talk with openly and share their innermost thoughts. How terrible, and what a change in less than ten years.

But while there are objective ways of measuring loneliness, loneliness is a very subjective experience. As such, it can be difficult to pin down or measure. In addition, we all have a different threshold for its effects. In other words, people's need for the company of others varies considerably.

A work colleague of mine, Louise, was out almost every evening socializing. Louise was a tall, attractive young woman who enjoyed amateur dramatics, had a small allotment, and was also a volunteer at a young persons' befriending group. But one cold winter she had a heavy cold and lost her voice afterwards. This meant she couldn't keep up with the amateur dramatics or the befriending group, as she had been told to rest her vocal cords for three months. During these three winter months, with no allotment to visit either, she gradually grew more and more lonely. Louise had a high need to be in the company of other people, so she could very easily find herself feeling lonely, as had happened here.

In contrast, another colleague, Alexander, who was about the same age as Louise, enjoyed nothing better than listening to music, was a skilled artist and had the most wonderful collection of tropical fish you've ever seen. Though he was a most articulate and interesting man, Alexander's need for others' company was considerably less, and so he was much less likely to feel lonely than Louise.

So we're all made differently – not better or worse, just differently. The majority of people will probably fit somewhere between Louise and Alexander in how much they need the company of other people.

## Time to make a change

Loneliness can last for a split second, or a minute, hours, days or more. An occasional brush with loneliness for a few hours or even a week or two is part of being human, and an increasingly common side effect of the varied and changing lifestyle most of us have today. It's part of life, and usually passes as a new job, a new area or a new relationship becomes familiar. But loneliness which persists for longer than this and begins to build upon itself is best dealt with.

If loneliness has persisted for a while, it can feel like moving a mountain to consider doing something about it. You may feel you just don't have the energy, or the motivation. You may feel rejected and useless. Maybe you tried before, and perhaps made some improvements, but then found that things just didn't work out for you. But hang on in there. It's worth it. The benefits can be absolutely life-changing.

It might help to use the old sayings like 'Tomorrow is the first day of the rest of your life'. Or 'You can't win the race if you're not in it'.

Remember the one about the longest journey beginning with a single step? Breaking away from loneliness most certainly begins with a small and manageable first step. And you'll find many to choose from in this book.

## When you are feeling lonely

First, what to do if you feel lonely right now. You may feel as if there's nothing you can do and that the very suggestion is adding insult to injury, but experts agree that combating loneliness isn't as hard as you may think. Professor John Cacioppo of the University of Chicago (of whom more later, in Chapter 4), a world authority on loneliness, advocates reaching out in small ways to those around you – to make more eye contact where appropriate, to say hello to someone at the shops or library, to undertake voluntary work, and generally to start opening your life in small, relatively risk-free ways before trying for committed and fulfilling friendships. Resist the urge to curl up in bed or on the sofa. Be pro-active – go out and treat yourself to a really good coffee, take the initiative and say hello to other people in the café or to the proprietor of the local shop. Talking to others, even if you don't need to and don't feel like it, is good practice. Comment on the weather to the deliveryman or the postwoman, or chat to people in the post office queue.

## Reach out

Even just going for a walk along the same route at the same time every day, or visiting the same shop for a paper, or getting the same bus or train, will mean that you gradually get to know the people you see every day, and before you know it there's a smile of recognition, then a nod and then perhaps a word about the weather, and so on. I still have many friends I met this way when taking my children to playgroup, nursery classes or school. A friend of mine, Mandy, met her husband Paolo as they walked to work in opposite directions along the same road every morning. A smile became a nod, then a 'hi', then a few words exchanged, and pretty soon a first date. They have now been married for nearly 20 years.

There's nothing new in this, of course – it's the way human beings and society have always operated. It's just that in our day and age, we sometimes have to re-learn these ancient customs. So don't wait until those familiar feelings of desolation take hold. Take action straight away.

## Simple ways to reach out

- Do something for someone else. This can really help. Make that call or visit to a friend who's having a rough time, check on an elderly or disabled neighbour, fill that charity bag and take it down to the shop.
- Check your e-mail or surf the net in an internet café or local library instead of the empty spare room, and say hello to the people around you.
- Read your book or magazine in a busy park among other people, instead of in your favourite armchair at home.
- When you're out, use positive body language if you want to elicit a response from others. Don't keep your head down. Hold your head high, put on a smile or say hello even if you don't feel like it, and see how others react. You'll get smiles and greetings back, I guarantee it.
- Even if you have a washing machine, do your washing at the launderette now and then. On the same basis, take a bus instead of driving. The chat is usually guaranteed to make you forget yourself and your own worries.
- Instead of phoning or e-mailing friends or relatives, go and see them, or ask them round for coffee. Suggest regular events such as playing computer games or chess, watching a film and having a pizza, or starting a reading club.
- Go to a museum, exhibition or public building such as a castle or stately home. If there's a tour, put your name down and make a point of chatting to others as you look round.
- Look in your local paper for any local events. I glanced through my local paper today, and there was an Open Door day at a local Norman church, a craft fair, an antiques and collectibles fair, a local farmers' market, a 'ghost walk', a classic car exhibition and a football match, all within easy reach.

## Walking

Walking is our most natural form of exercise and has tradition-ally been used as an easy problem-solver – *solvitur ambulando*, it is solved by walking, as the old Latin phrase says (attributed to St Augustine). The actual mechanisms of why walking helps you think more clearly are not fully understood, but studies have shown that this easy, repetitive activity does improve brain activity, as does any exercise. One study of people with epilepsy found that the abnormal brainwaves recorded on their electroencephalograms (EEGs) disappeared when they walked with heavy packs on their backs.

Walking has several benefits for the lonely person. It means you get out of the house, which improves mood and fitness as well as increasing the likelihood of seeing people. You're less likely to comfort eat and drink – proven dangers to the lonely person – if you're out taking a stroll. And, done with a friend or a group, it can be a social activity which is perfect for banishing loneliness.

Of course, not everyone likes to go for a walk, and not everyone has somewhere nice to walk. But even if the countryside isn't at your doorstep, towns and cities still provide opportunities for walking – indeed, some people prefer them. 'I need streets,' said Dickens, an inveterate walker and people-watcher.

## What about a pet?

A bit of a cliché for the lonely, but pet-ownership does have a three-fold bonus. The presence and companionship of a pet in the home reduces loneliness, lowers stress and also makes it more likely that you'll make more friends and acquaintances. If you walk a dog regularly, you will have more chance conversations than if you were walking alone. It's also been known for many years that stroking a friendly animal can lower your blood pressure. And their affectionate greetings, thirst for attention, need for regular feeding and unconditional love reduce feelings of being alone, and boost self-esteem and feelings of autonomy.

There has been much research carried out on the subject of pets. Findings have confirmed that having a cat or dog as a companion cushions the effects of stressful life events such as bereavement or divorce, and lessens anxiety, loneliness and depression.

One study in the journal *Hypertension* looked at stockbrokers – who have notoriously high levels of work stress – who were taking medication for high blood pressure. Half of the stockbrokers got a pet, and six months later researchers found that while medication helped lower resting blood pressure, only pet-ownership mitigated the spike in blood pressure that occurs during mental stress.

Even if you don't have a dog or cat of your own but have one as a regular visitor, you'll still have some of these benefits. This is why the practice of pets visiting hospitals and care homes is becoming more widespread. Many US penal institutions have found that using dogs has improved psychological well-being and rehabilitation of inmates. The prisoner has to look after the dog and train it for a particular purpose, such as becoming a guide dog.

### If you have to be alone

- Do something active. Anything will do: have a shower, do some gardening or housework. Wash up, clean your shoes, take the rubbish out, clear out a drawer. Re-organize your wardrobe or your furniture. Play a keep-fit DVD or try another active computer program. Don't spend time choosing what to do. Go for a jog or a swim, go to the gym or take a brisk walk. Doesn't matter what it is, as long as it's physical activity. Just moving around and doing something alters your brain chemistry and will help to keep the lonely feelings at bay. Don't forget to smile or say hello to people you may meet en route.
- Have a project on the go, such as learning a language or doing some study. Create a space or a desk with books and other tools you might need, so you always have somewhere to go and something to do when at a loss.
- Plan little treats such as a magazine, materials for a hobby you've always wanted to try, or ingredients for a delicious meal. Better still, invite someone to join you for the meal. Even if a friendship has drifted, people are likely to respond positively.
- Use social media to connect with others, but limit your time on-line and be discriminating. Focus on contacting those with common interests, say, rather than those who also feel lonely. There's some evidence to show that loneliness is contagious and can be transmitted via social networks – certainly, the last thing you want on a lonely Saturday night is to be reading depressing and negative on-line conversations.
- Sometimes it may help to see if there's anything underlying the

loneliness that needs addressing. This *doesn't* mean exploring any 'personality defects' – research has shown again and again that, although people blame themselves for being lonely and feel 'there must be something wrong with me', this isn't the case. But sometimes people are not the cure for loneliness and there may be other life issues underlying your feelings. Is the loneliness really about people or is there something else troubling you, such as an old unfulfilled ambition, that needs to be explored or expressed? Are you grieving for a specific person or situation and feel you just can't face other people yet? Write any thoughts down in your notebook or in a journal.

- Indulge in solitude – listen to music or go for a walk and be alert for simple sights – a robin with a feather in its beak, a child stomping in puddles, a changing sky on a wet afternoon. Enjoy the moment, because if you follow the suggestions in this book you might one day be looking back and wishing for some precious time alone!

- Use the solitude for meditation. This doesn't have to be demanding. Just sit in the silence, or with music if you prefer. The Quakers have a practice called 'centring down' or entering into a deep stillness or meditative state, while silence and meditation form an important part of Buddhist practices. The benefits are well documented.

## What not to do

- Avoid using alcohol or food to make yourself feel better. Or buying things you don't really need. These may give you an immediate lift, but this will only be short-term and you'll feel worse again when it wears off. It is all too easy to get into the habit of using alcohol or food or shopping to lessen the effects of being lonely, but this can lead to alcohol, debt, clutter or weight problems which you could do without. If you come across someone who feels the way you do, be each other's 'buddy', so that you have someone to call for support whenever temptation strikes.

- But it's important not to fall into the 'misery loves company' trap. Don't spend too much time with negative people, or those who drain your energy – people who have chronic emotional or life problems but who have no serious intention of doing anything about them. While commiserating and comfort are important, it's also vital to gravitate towards positive people.

- Don't give up. Look on it as a long-term project, and keep trying even if your first attempts are not very successful – you may be expecting too much of yourself and others. It's all a learning experience. No failures, only feedback to use another day.
- Don't expect other people to be a panacea or to solve everything. Remember to balance company with solitude, and look at Chapter 5 for ways in which this can be done.
- Don't make on-line social life a substitute for face-to-face acquaintances.

## If you need support right now

If you are feeling extremely lonely right now and think you need more support than this book can offer, there are many people you can reach out to for help, advice or support. For every problem or worry there is a support group or specialist adviser out there. This might be:

- a qualified counsellor;
- a doctor;
- a health visitor or practice nurse;
- a lawyer;
- the Citizens Advice Bureau;
- a priest or minister;
- specialist support groups such as a befriending group, Victim Support, Age UK, Alcoholics Anonymous, the Samaritans, a business support network, Rape Crisis, a cancer support organization, Women's Aid. These and others are listed at the end of the book, and there are many more.

So don't be alone, if you need to reach out to someone now: make that call or e-mail and find your way out of that unhappy place. There are many, many people out there who can help, who may have ideas and solutions you haven't thought about. If you've suffered some kind of trauma such as an accident, assault, sexual abuse or bereavement, it can be even more important to get professional help from someone who understands. A traumatic event often leaves the person with a burden of shame, which plays its part in cutting him or her off from the rest of humanity and makes it hard to seek help. Bear in mind that professionals will have heard much worse. It is their job to act in confidence, with broad and accepting minds.

## Summary

Loneliness is widespread, in all age groups and backgrounds. It's not just a problem for older people. One in ten of us often feel lonely.

- There are different kinds of loneliness. Social loneliness may be felt if you lack a satisfying social network; emotional loneliness may result if you don't have an intimate attachment with a friend or partner, or if you have a yearning, such as for a child or grandchild, or for a particular place or time.
- Loneliness is an individual experience and can have a wide range of effects. Anyone can be lonely, including the rich and famous.
- Everyone will probably feel lonely at some time in their life.
- If you need support right now, there are people out there who can help. Consider professional help if need be.

# 2

## Changing society

Because of previous bad experiences, many people have lost social confidence. This might be because of a long period of enforced solitude, lack of social practice or just plain shyness, all of which mean that meeting and talking to people has become more of an effort. But as this chapter shows, this isn't the whole story. Major changes to the way we live are putting more and more people at risk of loneliness in the UK today, according to Andrew McCulloch, Chief Executive of the MHF. Nearly half of those in the MHF's study *The Lonely Society?* thought that people were becoming lonelier in general. Social changes are another reason why people shouldn't blame themselves for being lonely. Often, it's the opportunity to make friends and get out and about socially that's the problem.

Living alone is probably the most obvious situation linked to loneliness, and according to the MHF report twice as many people in the UK are now living alone compared with just four decades ago. The report estimates that 12 per cent of UK residents are now living alone, which amounts to over seven million people. Approximately one in eight homes in the average street has just one occupant. In the USA, the position is similar, with the numbers living alone having risen by a fifth in just ten years. There are a number of reasons for this change.

### Careers and employment

In today's complex world, moving from job to job and working long hours makes for a lifestyle that doesn't leave time for keeping up friendships and contact with family, or making new friends. According to the Mental Health Foundation, major changes since 1990 mean that young people are increasingly moving away from their home communities to seek work and to progress along their career path. The report also indicates that many of us are working longer hours just to pay the bills or to maintain an affluent lifestyle, missing out on time to see friends and family, put down roots and generally establish long-term friendships.

You may find yourself with a small and narrow network of contacts, such as work colleagues or neighbours, which you lose if you have to move job or house again. Also, many young people are leaving it later to settle down with a partner, and others are choosing not to have a partner at all. Some of those who do leave it later in life can't find a partner when they do eventually decide it's time to settle down.

The days of a 'job for life' are long gone. The current average number of jobs we hold in our lifetimes in the UK is now six and rising. And with pension age increasing, the chances of having to move job and house are only going to increase likewise. In some areas of work, there is a belief that staying too long in one job is detrimental to an overall career path. This puts more pressure on people to move around. Here are some interesting statistics:

- In 2000, from a UK study of over 9,000 people aged between 16 and 69, the Department of Social Security found that those between ages 60 and 69 had had an average of six different jobs, in three or more industries, in the course of their lifetime. Each younger generation had tended to have been in more jobs, staying in each for less time. Those in their 20s had already been in four jobs.
- The Bureau of Labor Statistics in the USA reported in 2008 that people born between 1957 and 1964 had held an average of 10.8 jobs between the ages of 18 and 42. There was little difference between men and women in these figures.

### Shift work

If you work nightshift or rotating shifts, or have a very early start in the morning, you can find yourself at odds with everyone else when it comes to socializing or getting involved in activities. Who wants to go out for a drink and a chat at 7.30 in the morning when you're just finishing work? Finding a Zumba dance class or a football match or being able to hit the shops with friends is also very difficult at the times you can make it. And a weekly commitment is hopeless if your shifts rotate endlessly.

## Other working practices

Problems can also arise for off-shore workers, or those in the armed services or merchant navy who are away from home for weeks or months at a time, and then home solidly for a week or even for several months.

Those who work alone for many hours are at an obvious disadvantage too: farmers, lorry drivers, delivery van drivers, and workmen who are given the house key and left to work alone on decorating, plumbing or electrical work. Then there are salespeople who cover vast territories, finding themselves driving miles each day and sleeping in a different hotel every evening. The same could be said of actors, musicians and performers of all kinds, who can be on tour all over the country and abroad. Consultants also have a similar solitary existence, making establishing roots and a social life well down their priority list. Executives and managers are moved around the country and the world, to the detriment of their own social lives and those of their children. Some couples may have jobs hundreds of miles apart and yet still have a home together. Or maybe one partner works away Monday to Friday, with the other staying in the family home, and they only meet up as a family at weekends. This leaves each partner with more time alone than they would prefer, and this can be a lonely existence Monday to Friday.

## Divorce and separation

The MHF report also suggests that the doubling of the divorce rate over the last four decades has been a contributory factor in this increase in people living alone. Divorce and separation may cut you off from friends who were also your partner's friends, or from your own friends who find things awkward and don't know what to say. You're no longer a couple, and many invitations are for couples. More about separation and relationship breakdown in Chapters 6 and 7.

## If you've lost touch with friends or family

It's remarkably easy to lose touch with friends and family. School friends used to remain friends for life, in the days when most people left school and took a job in their local area. This gave tremendous stability, with school friends growing up and starting out in life alongside each other, and with friends from work always around too. Now, with each move, even the steps from school to university and from university into the workplace, there's a tendency to lose touch with more friends, family and colleagues, and the length of any new acquaintance becomes shorter.

## Older people

According to the Campaign to End Loneliness, 51 per cent of those over 75 live alone, and 11 per cent of older people see their family, friends or neighbours less than once a month. They also estimate that, currently, one million people aged over 65 are often or always lonely.

## Social media

Social media are a bit of a mixed blessing. For those who can't get out easily – such as people with disabilities, parents of young children, and carers – Facebook, MySpace, Twitter and LinkedIn can be a godsend. Research shows that people who use the internet to boost and enrich face-to-face relationships also benefit. It's when people start using it as a total substitute for 'live relationships' that they become lonelier and more depressed. So the internet makes a good servant but a poor master.

This said, I do believe that any kind of contact from other people helps to relieve loneliness, from phone calls to texting and e-mail. I can certainly feel at the end of a day filled with phone calls and e-mails not that I've been in the office all day, but rather as if I've been part of a busy community of friends and co-workers around the country. It's that feeling of being part of a group that makes the difference. That said, the 2010 Mental Health Foundation report on loneliness discovered that one in eight people admitted to spending too much time chatting to friends on-line when they should be seeing them personally. It's all about balance. An on-line or 'virtual' social world shouldn't be a substitute for physical contact with others, but it can complement a social network, and it's much better if the alternative is no contact at all. I do know people who are on social networking sites such as Facebook and Twitter for hours at a time, and this does make you think that that time would be better spent actually going out and meeting people.

But the internet, used carefully, has so much available to energize and motivate you, and to keep you in touch with other people and the world outside – news sites, e-mail, Skype, social networking sites, Twitter, discussion forums, help-lines, playing chess with a friend on-line, downloading music, a wealth of information to keep you interested and busy. A tentative step into the virtual world may be an easy first move towards getting out and about again in the real world. Ian Rankin, the well-known writer of the 'Rebus' series of detective books, confesses to being a frequent user of Twitter, and says that as he works from home and works alone, Twitter connects him to the outside world and he feels as if he's in a huge airy office full of clever and witty people. He has also made new friends in his home town of Edinburgh and beyond through 'tweeting', and has organized activities on-line which then took place in the 'real' world.

I was recently invited to a friend's on-line book launch. This just meant dropping into the author's 'blog' page and leaving a message, usually some good wishes and a favourable comment about the book. The author could then reply to this message in real time. Reading all the comments others had left, and the author's responses, did make me feel as if I had had a real social interaction with many people I knew, though I hadn't actually left my office at all. It's unlikely that so many people would have had time to attend an actual event of this kind, and I wouldn't have had a chance to hear what everyone had to say.

## The rise of BACS and the supermarket

Surprising causes of loneliness! However, direct payments into banks via BACS would seem to make for a lonelier society. In

*Sons and Lovers*, D.H. Lawrence paints a vivid picture of a small boy collecting wages for his father on a Friday night in provincial Nottingham, entailing a host of social interactions. Such days are long gone. Benefits, including Child Benefit, and pensions are paid directly into the bank, so there is no longer a need to go out to collect this money, and in the process to meet friends and neighbours or at least have a chat with the nice lady behind the post office counter, who knows your name both from your benefit book and because she sees you every week. Likewise, the rise of the all-embracing supermarket, and other similar superstores, has led to the decline of the corner shop, and many local post offices have had to close their doors too. The daily trip for a newspaper or some bread meant meeting acquaintances on the way, chatting with people in the shop, and then talking over the fence to your neighbours on the way back. An invitation for a coffee from a friend you met in the shop could take up the afternoon. Sadly, these social interactions are disappearing all too fast.

## Summary

- Twice as many people live alone today as compared with 40 years ago.
- One in every eight UK homes has only one person living in it.
- Many current career and job priorities and choices make loneliness more likely.
- Other social factors increase the incidence of loneliness today, including changes in the way we work, a rise in the rates of divorce and separation, and increased geographical mobility.

# 3

# Not alone, but lonely

A particular kind of emotional loneliness is when you're not alone but still have an inner feeling of being alone. It's not a question here of lack of human contact, but of an emotional state of not feeling connected to other people. This type of loneliness you carry round with you. It's a perceived isolation that may not be assuaged by the presence of other people, and indeed consists of a strong sense that your relationships do not meet your needs. There are many situations in which people can feel lonely in a crowd.

## An unhappy marriage or relationship

Thousands of people each day feel trapped in an unhappy or unfulfilling marriage or relationship. This can be an acutely lonely existence which, if not addressed, can destroy what relationship there is and lead to other problems such as depression. This kind of loneliness may be rooted in the misconception that simply having a relationship or getting married will automatically cure loneliness. In fact, this assumption may lead some people to enter into emotional commitments that merely deepen their loneliness. In the book *The Mirages of Marriage* (W.W. Norton, 1968), authors William J. Lederer and Don D. Jackson note that 'the most intense and excruciating loneliness is the loneliness that is shared with another person'. If a relationship fails to meet a person's social needs, resentment and emotional withdrawal may result, in turn leading to increased loneliness.

You may feel lonely in a marriage or relationship for a variety of reasons, such as emotional abuse or jealousy, a lack of physical intimacy or the demands of work. After the first exciting flush of love, you may have discovered you just don't function on the same intellectual, sexual or ideological level. Or with both of you working and a family to bring up, you hardly get a chance to talk

21

and relate to each other as a couple any more. You may simply have grown apart. Sometimes you stay together for the children or for appearances, because you're scared or simply because you've no confidence, nowhere else to go and no money to start a new life. So you put up with the lack of love, the affairs, the selfishness, the drudgery or even the physical or mental abuse.

Sometimes people can place too high an expectation on a partner and on their relationship. Perhaps this is because of the heady romantic imagery we see and hear all around us from an early age, and the numerous films and books which paint a rosy picture in which the relationship is paramount in your life and meets all of your needs, and indeed allows you to 'live happily ever after'. But the reality can be quite different. It's not that a relationship can't be exciting, wonderful and all you hoped for, and grow and develop as time goes on. But it can't fill your entire life, and your partner can't meet all of your needs in life. That's too much to expect. You still need friends, something to believe in, and interests and challenges outside your relationship, to run alongside it and nurture it, keeping it strong and healthy. Some research has shown that, for married women, female friends may sometimes provide more emotional connection than is possible in a male–female relationship – or at least supplement it – because women tend to listen to each other with more empathy and attention than do men.

Relationship loneliness carries particular dangers, according to experts, leading to depression and self-destructive behaviour such as addiction or infidelity. Women in particular may feel pushed towards infidelity because of feeling lonely and unfulfilled in their current relationship, says clinical psychologist Dr Joyce Hamilton Berry, of Washington, DC. High levels of stress in a relationship also increase the risk of sleeping problems and depression. And in his book *Addiction and Change* (Guilford Press, 2003), Carlo C. DiClemente, professor of psychology at the University of Maryland, Baltimore, points out how some women may use drugs and alcohol as coping mechanisms rather than face emotional difficulties and stress in their relationships. They may also feel disconnected from their families and friends, increasing any emotional instability – and loneliness.

There can also be loneliness at the start of a relationship, for example when you decide to live together. If this means leaving your childhood home, mother, father, brothers and sisters, that whole way of life, and the dog and cat to boot, some people will miss all these familiar things, and there will be an adjustment period before they settle in. Even if you've been living on your own, you'll have been making your own decisions, enjoying your own space and doing your own thing, and you can miss that too. Many of us expect that the new romance, falling in love and our new partner will fill our life and make us complete, but no one person, however wonderful and no matter how much we love him or her, can do all of that. An important relationship is still something new coming into your already well-established life. It's not wiping out your old life and starting again. But any feeling of loneliness or even homesickness at the start will usually pass as this new and exciting part of your life with your partner becomes more familiar and you re-assign a place in your heart and your world for those old familiarities such as parents, siblings, your old duvet cover and even the family pet.

## Lonely through loss

The most acute feelings of loneliness hit us when we lose someone precious to us. Each of us goes through this in our own way, as befits such a very personal loss. The loneliness is of a deep and painful kind, which stays with us like an unwelcome companion and leaves an indelible mark on us. I can honestly say my world changed for ever when I lost both my mother and my father-in-law within a month of each other. And even in a busy shopping mall, or the hubbub of visiting a group of friends, there is a part of me that still feels that loneliness and that loss.

Strong and painful feelings of loss are a natural reaction to losing a partner, parent or friend, whether the person has died or has moved away, or your relationship has broken up or changed its dynamic in some way. Losing access to your children as the result of a divorce or separation is a critical loss. For some, the death of a pet can produce major feelings of loss and emptiness.

## Other losses

But feelings of loss and grief can also come from losing a way of life, or longing for a particular time or era. You may be yearning for the freedom of student days, or a time in your life when you were better off financially, or when you were happier, or more physically fit and mobile. The feeling of having an 'empty nest' isn't just about the absence of children after they've flown the nest. It's also about the loss of a long-established and familiar daily and weekly way of life. This kind of grief can also involve a loss of identity and purpose.

There are many other ways a loss of identity can come about, through losing a job or a place on a committee, or by growing out of something which used to fit like a glove. For example, the man who's played football since he was a child, and then finds his sporting days ended by injury, ill health or simply becoming older. Or the woman who resigns from running the local music festival through lack of time or energy, or just because it's time to let someone else have a go. A large hole appears in your life, and you're not at all sure how to fill it. Loss of identity often comes with a loss in status, especially if you've lost your job. You may have many friends and a loving partner, but other people won't necessarily provide what's missing. To achieve this, you may have to branch out more, try new life challenges and new interests. You'll find more suggestions on how to do this in later chapters.

## When you're worried

Being worried about someone or something can be a very isolating experience. Especially when negative consequences are likely and there's no-one you can talk to about it, this can produce both anxiety and loneliness. Here are two typical cases I've come across.

> Mary, 37, suspects one of her friends, Jennifer, is drinking too much, and is worried she is becoming dependent. But she doesn't want to mention it to any of her other friends in case she's wrong and Jennifer finds out and becomes angry and falls out with her.

> Dev, who has just celebrated his fortieth birthday, noticed by accident that a very respected work colleague, Geoff, has over-claimed his expenses by a substantial amount. It looks deliberate to Dev, and

he knows Geoff is having financial problems at the moment after his divorce. Dev doesn't know what to do. Maybe it was a mistake.

If these two situations aren't resolved quickly, Mary and Dev would benefit from talking to an objective and trustworthy sounding-board. You'll find a range of contact details at the end of the book. There's no reason why anyone should have to cope with dilemmas like these on their own.

We all have a serious issue to face at some time in our lives – anything from a debt problem to health matters, being bullied, a divorce, an assault or a car accident. Or perhaps an important business venture has failed, or you've lost your job, or there's a court case to contend with. Even if you already have a counsellor, a lawyer or a consultant of some kind to talk to every week or every month, the rest of the time you may be feeling very alone with this nagging worry that has suddenly dropped into your previously comfortable world. Speaking to others who know what you're going through can help. This needn't be face to face; most support groups have phone or e-mail support, or a 'discussion board' on their website where you can read others' contributions and experiences, or post a question or comment yourself, anonymously if you prefer.

## If you have a secret

If you have a secret you'd rather not have, the world can seem a very empty place, with no-one out there to turn to for support or to share the unwanted burden. I know two people who found themselves in this unenviable position.

Carole, aged 31, was sexually abused by her step-father for a year before she left home to go to university. She told no-one about this. She is now in a long-term relationship with a very supportive partner whom she loves very much. But she has many empty lonely moments with her secret; she wants to share it with her partner but thinks she could lose him if she does.

Andy is 16, still at school and a keen footballer, and is sure that he is gay. He's always felt this, ever since he can remember. But he has told no-one, and feels totally alone.

As with Dev and Mary above, Carole and Andy could relieve their anxiety and loneliness by talking things over with someone like a specialist counsellor, or a trusted friend or relative. They could also start by talking to their GP if that's easier, and GPs will have details about who to contact.

## In your job

If you dislike your job or your colleagues, or it's just the kind of job where people don't have a chance to talk and interact with each other, the feeling of isolation can be very strong, without feelings of support and belonging. Or maybe you're being bullied or victimized, or you have a line manager or colleague who is unnecessarily critical or dismissive. With the bills to be paid you can't just leave, and you can't be too picky if jobs are scarce. Food is needed on the table. But there are things you can do and people who can help. If there is an occupational health adviser or employee assistance programme (EAP), you can usually talk to someone in confidence about problems like stress or bullying, or poor relationships with colleagues. And you can always be on the look-out for a job you would prefer. Even in difficult economic times, jobs do come up.

Life changes such as redundancy or retirement may also make for loneliness, not just for the person whose job ends but also for his or her partner. Less income may mean fewer opportunities for socializing, or having one partner around the house all day may curtail the social activities of the other partner.

## If you have many acquaintances, but no real friends

Fiona used to live a few streets away from me, and I would often bump into her when she was out walking her lovely Labrador dog, named Tara. She always came across as friendly, with a comfortable way with people, and always had a story to tell about this or that or what she'd been doing that week. She was always busy, out and about, always chatting to someone in the street or in the supermarket, and I assumed she had a circle of close friends, although she lived alone. But then one day she said quite suddenly to me, 'You know, I was just thinking: I have lots and lots of acquaintances, people I know a bit. Must be as many as 50 or 60. But I have no real friends, no-one close. No-one I can really share things with. Isn't that strange?'

This touched my heart, and opened my mind still further to the great variety of human experience and how you should never judge a book by its cover.

## Friendships have to be fulfilling

Lots of friends but still lonely? Maybe they are the wrong friends, who take and don't give. Friendship has to go both ways equally, give and take. All taking and no giving leaves you feeling more and more drained and empty, and feeling lonely, like when you have coffee with a friend who just chatters on and on about him or herself, or if you have a friend who manipulates you or makes you feel guilty. So you need to begin to set limits on this kind of friendship. There will be more on types of friendships and making friends in Chapter 7, and more in Chapter 10 on how to develop a better sense of self-worth, and in this way attract people who want to give as well as take.

## Looking after children

Even with two parents, bringing up children is a 24/7 commitment. Children will talk with you and play with you and around you, or the older ones will spend time in their rooms or out with friends. But they won't relate to you and interact with you as a person: it will be as Mum or Dad. And you're so much more than just Mum or Dad, and it's that other part of you that can feel lonely.

Bringing up children on your own can be one of the most demanding and tiring of lives. Yes, there are the rewards of a happy smiling child, and the freedom of a walk in the park, and the exhilarating laughter as they slide excitedly down the chute for the tenth time. But there is also the pressure of it all resting on your shoulders, with no-one to sound off to when the little one spills her juice all over the table again. And when the children are safely tucked up in bed at night, that quiet and emptiness can descend, and an aching loneliness with it.

## When your children leave home

Even though your partner is still with you and you have a good social life, when your last child leaves home, many parents, often mothers, experience the 'empty nest syndrome'. Just as it sounds, this is a feeling of emptiness and loneliness, a kind of separation anxiety similar to the feeling some parents have on their child's first day of school. After something like 18 years or more of knowing roughly where your child is and whether he or she is safe, fed, clothed appropriately, warm, or in bed at night, and well and not in need of a doctor or a bottle of cough mixture, there is suddenly nothing. All of that is gone all at once, not just the child. And this can feel like quite a sudden shock if you are not expecting it. When my youngest left home aged 21, I knew all about the 'empty nest' and thought I was prepared for it, working in a satisfying job, with a loving partner and a good circle of friends. But that feeling of emptiness still hit me like a bolt from the blue, and took some time to pass. Indeed, I still have moments of loneliness and miss each one of my children's constant presence around me, even though they are at the end of the phone, texts and e-mail, and visit often.

## Carers

The kind of loneliness you can feel sitting hour upon hour with a loved one who has dementia, and who sees you as a friendly stranger, can only be imagined unless you have experienced it for yourself. But any caring situation can be a lonely one, and each day can seem endless, particularly if you are yearning for a good night's sleep. In many situations, the loneliness may be compounded by the fact that there is little or no feedback from the person you are caring for.

## Health conditions or disability

Certain health conditions, such as heart disease, arthritis, epilepsy, eczema, lung disease and others, may create feelings of difference or isolation (as well as reducing actual social opportunities). So may disabilities, a hearing or sight impairment, or reduced mobility. The loneliness can be two-fold – as well as the 'lonely in a crowd' feeling we're talking about in this chapter, it can be more difficult to get out and about and meet friends. This may lead to a downward spiral of decreased outings and social contact, leading to even less social contact and even less need to leave the home to meet people: you could think of it as enforced social withdrawal.

Mental health problems can also cause people to be lonely. Conditions such as depression, anxiety or bipolar disorder by their very nature make socializing difficult. Phobias such as agoraphobia and social phobia are particularly debilitating in this respect. Friends can also find it difficult to keep up a relationship with someone who has a mental health problem, as they often can't find the words to say or don't know the right things to do.

## Students

In the past it was assumed that students leaving home to go to university would be having such a high old time that homesickness and loneliness just wouldn't enter the picture. But experiences of student counselling and support services over the years have not supported this. Despite being surrounded by peers, many students every year become lonely and homesick, some mildly but many to an extent which interferes with their studies. A number of students every year have to give up their studies entirely through devastating homesickness.

For some students, it can seem as if everyone around them is having a great time, laughing and joking, playing sport and social-izing, and as if they're the only one left out. So they imagine it must be their fault. They're just not good enough. No-one wants to know them. But of course none of that is true. It's not just them, and it's not because of being a wimp or not good friend material. Homesickness is very real and very distressing, and can affect anyone. I actually experienced it myself very strongly, not when I first went to university at 18, but when I went on a course at Sussex University when I was somewhat older, with a husband and two young children left at home.

## If you're abroad

People are much more mobile than ever before, and people from different cultures, ethnic backgrounds, faiths, sexual and social backgrounds are all living much more intertwined and interdependent lives than ever before in the UK, as in many other countries. So the world can seem like a different place, and you can feel lonely even when working in a busy town or university. You miss your culture, your way of life and just having a shared background with someone who connects with your accent, your language, way of life, special days, shared memories, and all the rest.

## Addictions

There are all sorts of substances human beings can become addicted to – sometimes physically, sometimes psychologically, sometimes both. Drugs, alcohol, tobacco, and so on. An addiction of this kind will have a devastating effect on any relationship.

## Poverty

You'll remember the words of Mother Teresa mentioned in the Introduction, which describe loneliness as the worst form of poverty. However, an underlying and often unrecognized reason for loneliness is poverty itself – a simple lack of the finances needed for socializing in the first place. Even having a cup of coffee and a cake with a friend is relatively expensive, and a lunch out or a day's shopping or bowling, or a visit to the seaside, is a serious financial consideration if you are living near or under the poverty line. Poverty has many and varied causes, such as unemployment, poor health and disability. Lone parents, too, are a particularly vulnerable group. And at the extreme end of this, those living in absolute poverty, such as the homeless, are almost certain to be lonely.

Poverty, then, has strong implications for our social existence. It may not seem much of an issue not to be able to go out for a meal with a friend but, if finances are stretched, the evidence suggests it would be wise to find other ways to socialize that don't involve spending so much money. Spending time with others isn't just an indulgence but a necessity, which may be biologically implanted in us. Why this is so important is something we'll consider in the next chapter.

## Summary

- A number of situations can cause that 'lonely in a crowd' feeling.
- Some typical situations which can produce this kind of loneliness include: an unhappy marriage or relationship; being a carer; looking after children; being unhappy at work; being worried; facing a serious health or other issue; keeping a difficult secret; or an 'empty nest'.

# 4

# Loneliness – a survival technique

Our need for social contact and support is fundamental to our emotional well-being, not just as individuals but as whole communities. It's rooted in the deep need human beings have for each other, and there is a great deal of research to suggest that loneliness evolved as a survival impulse that keeps people within the tribe to ensure the safety and reproduction of the species. So, far from being merely a private, personal matter, loneliness can be viewed as a common signal – just as hunger or thirst propels us to eat or drink, so loneliness propels us towards companionship. There may be extremes of appetite, in that some people need only a little occasional sustenance, whereas others need a daily feast – but the same social hungers exist in us all.

In other words, far from being a sign of personal failure, in evolutionary terms loneliness is 'an aversive signal whose purpose is to motivate us to reconnect', says neuroscientist John Cacioppo, professor of psychology at the University of Chicago and author of *Loneliness: Human nature and the need for social connection* (co-authored with William Patrick, former science editor at Harvard University Press; John Wiley, 2008).

Cacioppo is a founder of social neuroscience, which is based on the premise that we are a social species, rather than individuals, and that biological processes are linked to cultural influences. Social neuroscience looks at how the brain and its processes are involved with social interactions. Cacioppo explains that human biology 'has evolved within a fiercely social world . . . and is shaped profoundly by the social world'.

So, while people do often blame themselves for being lonely or feel that their loneliness is the result of an individual defect, social neuroscience says that this is nonsense – that would be like blaming yourself for becoming thirsty.

## Only connect

We have evolved as a social species over thousands of years, right from prehistoric times, when early human beings and their predecessors lived in strongly bonded social groups. This had a number of benefits, the three most important being protection, a ready supply of food, and successful reproduction. Groups with a strong social bond like this co-operate with each other, for example sharing tasks like food gathering and arranging shelter. They act in an 'altruistic' or unselfish way to others, behaviours that encourage the survival and well-being of those in the group. Thus, while loneliness may be painful on an individual basis, it serves a purpose for the species – if the individual strays too far from the group, unpleasant feelings of isolation propel him or her to rejoin it. Loneliness works as a kind of social glue.

If you trace back along the evolutionary track to our primate ancestors, strong social bonding and living in close-knit groups was the way of life for them all. The same is true of our current primate cousins such as chimpanzees, who live in groups of between 15 and 100 or more, all with some social bond with each other. That is, they all know one another, just the way we know other people. Scientists have shown that the social group is important to many other species including mice, rats, pigs, squirrel monkeys, rhesus monkeys, chimpanzees and rabbits. Exclusion from the group is an established punishment – the child sent out of the classroom and solitary confinement for the prisoner are two examples. Indeed, there's evidence that separation from the group has devastating effects in any social species – even fruit flies die earlier if isolated, whereas genetically damaged fruit flies live longer in the presence of other flies. Researchers at Ohio State University found that mice living with a partner had a better outcome after suffering a stroke than those who lived in social isolation – whereas living alone increased their chances of dying or of suffering more brain damage. So our need for others is basic. Our genes have pre-programmed us to behave in this way.

Ongoing social contact has particular importance in terms of propagating the species, which, for humans, entails years of dependence by children on their parents. Given that the human child is unable to look after itself when born and remains in need of care and support for many years, having a safe, secure place to grow up, where the child's parents are more likely to survive, is of obvious benefit to the species.

Today, we still come pre-programmed to survive. Developmental psychologist John Bowlby, founder of attachment theory, explored how we instinctively avoid isolation and stay close to others. Attachment theory looks at how infants form close bonds with their caregivers, and was some of the first work to involve evolutionary thinking about human social development. Our deep-rooted social instincts manifest in many ways – this, for example, is why we are so good at face recognition. Despite there being millions of us on the planet, many of us still never forget a face. Previously, it might have been a matter of life or death to be able to correctly identify others in your group. It's a survival skill implanted from birth – a human baby is born with a focal length just right to see his mother's face clearly as he feeds, ensuring her baby recognizes her from the earliest possible moment. Natural selection supported this kind of living as it made survival and raising a family much more successful.

So even though many of us now live in concrete towns and cities with street lighting, shopping malls and fast cars all around us, we still need to be with other people and have close social and intimate bonds with others. At the heart of it all we still feel the need to be part of a social group.

## Empathy

We might think of empathy as something special and rare, that we can only share with a selected few friends or with long-term partners. In fact, empathy can serve a working social purpose even in people who've just met, according to some research. One study found that, even without a shared past or social network, two strangers can strike up a rapport just by having a few things in common and can build a relationship in a five-minute conversation. The research showed much swifter bonding than expected in people who learned they shared interests such as a certain author or musical band. Priyanka Carr of Stanford University concluded,

'We're built to connect with other people. We're meant to have relationships, to feel what our partners feel.'

While empathy is common in couples who have been together for many years, the fact that it can also exist in couples who have only just met lends new meaning to the phenomenon of 'love at first sight'. This immediate emotional bond was shown to outstanding effect in the famous 1946 film *Brief Encounter*, directed by David Lean, in which Trevor Howard and Celia Johnson play two married strangers meeting by chance in a waiting room in a railway station and forming an immediate intense relationship with each other.

Interestingly, lack of empathy is one feature often supposed to distinguish those with autistic spectrum disorders (ASD). Some experts believe, however, that some ASD individuals may have not too little empathy but too much, which they are unable to process. According to autism expert and therapist Phoebe Caldwell, some people with autism are in fact oversensitive to the feelings of others, rather than insensitive, but cannot handle the emotional pain that an empathetic response entails, and so have learnt to suppress their feelings of empathy.

Andrew McCulloch, chief executive of the Mental Health Foundation, agrees that human beings are social animals and that we have evolved to live in an extended group. Not being part of such a group can lead to feelings of anxiety and depression. The MHF report found that 47 per cent of the women and 37 per cent of the men they talked to had felt depressed owing to loneliness. In addition to having an adverse effect on mental health, loneliness can affect your physical health, too.

## Loneliness and health

Research has shown that lack of social support militates against health in a number of ways. People who don't have enough social support in their lives become increasingly vulnerable to tension and stress. Lonely people report higher levels of stress, even when exposed to the same stressors as the non-lonely and even when they are relaxing. In addition, lonely people tend to be more negative in their expectations of social interactions, and the encounters they do have tend to be less fulfilling than those of the non-lonely and do not buffer them from stress as relationships normally do. Lonely people tend to brace themselves against 'social threats' via a mindset which finds greater fault with themselves and with others. They often expect others to be less friendly – self-created expectations which paradoxically often have a way of fulfilling themselves.

In studies using functional MRI (fMRI) scans, the brains of the lonely and of the non-lonely respond in different ways in terms of social perception. When looking at pictures of happy social situations, for example, lonely people have less activity in a part of the brain that normally lights up in association with reward, making them more likely to seek comfort in non-social rewards.

In practical terms, all this means that without friends, family or a partner to talk to and share your day with, it becomes more difficult to cope with the daily hassles and stresses of life. This in turn can, in the long run, make you more prone to ill health. Bear in mind that we're talking more about chronic loneliness here, rather than transient episodes of feeling alone. Of course, everyone is likely to have periods of loneliness in their life. Indeed, as we've seen, this may serve a purpose at key times of a person's life – after a move, say, or being widowed, when, in due course, loneliness prompts the person to begin to reach out to others again. But long term, untackled loneliness is likely to have harmful effects.

Research has pinpointed a number of ways in which health may be affected:

- *Greater risk of heart disease.* Stressed and lonely people tend to have higher levels of cortisol, a hormone released in response to stress. A persistent stressful state can result in general wear and tear on the cardiovascular system, according to research by Professor John Cacioppo. Another study at the University of Pittsburgh School of Medicine linked feeling lonely to a nearly 80 per cent increase in the risk of heart disease in women. And a different study in 2006, of people aged 50 to 68, found that those who scored highest for loneliness also had higher blood pressure.
- *Problems with sleep, in particular with achieving deep sleep.* Sleep tends to be less restful and restorative because of mini awakenings throughout the night. Even though the person may not

remember these in the morning they are, according to Cacioppo, the brain's ancient warning system kicking in, reminding the lonely of their vulnerability, especially when defenceless and asleep.

- *Cognitive effects.* There's also evidence that loneliness affects cognitive function, contributing to the development of Alzheimer's disease. One study found that the risk of Alzheimer's disease was double in the lonely, compared with those who were not lonely.
- *Effect on the immune system.* For example, in addition to Cacioppo's work, research at Carnegie Mellon University in Pennsylvania found that lonely and socially isolated first-year students had a weaker immune response to flu injections than did other students. A study at the University of California found that social isolation also had a biological effect on the immune system, increasing the inflammatory response which is the immune system's first response to infection, and weakening the body's ability to fight viruses.

Loneliness may affect your health in other ways, too; for example, if you're depressed, or even out of the habit of connecting with others, you may neglect symptoms and not visit the doctor, so missing a medical condition. One survey even suggested that doctors themselves admit that they provide better or more complete medical care to patients who have supportive families and are not socially isolated.

There's also evidence that social disconnection contributes to poor health behaviours, such as a bad diet. Lonely people tend to consume more calories, to comfort eat more fats and sugars, and to drink too much alcohol. In some cases, alcoholism and drug addiction are dangers. The lonely exercise less, and are more likely to give up exercise. When there's no-one to tell you not to take that extra chocolate or glass of wine or to urge you to come out for a walk, it's just so much easier to reach for another chocolate or another drink, and to stay curled up on the sofa watching television or playing computer games. It appears that loneliness affects our ability to control thoughts, emotions and impulses. It reduces will-power, self-control and perseverance, thus skewing the ability to follow a healthy lifestyle. In all, in his ongoing research,

Cacioppo found that the difference between a lonely person and a more gregarious person was, staggeringly, akin to 'a smoker and a non-smoker'.

## The feedback loop

In their book, John Cacioppo and William Patrick suggest that loneliness creates a feedback loop that reinforces social anxiety, fear and other negative feelings. Combined with some of the statistics and information in this chapter, this may sound rather daunting. Is there an escape from loneliness? Yes, say Cacioppo and Patrick, and it starts with awareness of what is going on:

- Realize that loneliness is a signal – the pain of loneliness indicates that something needs to change.
- Start recognizing the 'loneliness loop'. Understand that loneliness can take on a life of its own, creating negative feedback which reinforces feelings of being a social failure.
- Be aware of the negative impact long-term loneliness may have on mental and physical health.
- Reach out – start overcoming the fear of connecting with others, even in small ways, as explained in Chapter 1.
- Think positive. Lonely people can get into the habit of expecting rejection, so start expecting the best in your relationships.

At the beginning of this chapter we looked at loneliness in terms of it being a basic instinct, such as hunger. Cacioppo says that indeed 'Lonely people feel a hunger. The key is to realize that the solution lies not in being fed, but in cooking for and enjoying a meal with others.'

On the same premise, though, we don't need to eat all the time! This chapter has looked at the need for social contact – conversely, the next chapter discusses our need for solitude, and how to make the most of being alone.

## Summary

- Human beings are naturally social, and have evolved over millions of years living in close social groups because this increased the chances of survival.
- Loneliness is a signal to us that we should seek the company of others. It is therefore nothing to be ashamed of.
- Chronic loneliness may affect your health.
- Constant loneliness may reinforce social anxiety, and the cure is reaching out. Time spent with other people helps to keep you healthy in mind, body and spirit.

# 5

# Loneliness versus solitude

Most people need solitude sometimes. I certainly do. This need varies from one person to another, from my minimum of half an hour each day to many hours a day. If I had a free choice, I would probably prefer three to four hours to myself every day. Being alone gives a sense of freedom and respite, and room for the imagination to grow.

Some people simply prefer their own company most of the time. Hill-walkers, cyclists and long-distance runners often travel alone. Painters can work alone for many hours at their easel in order to get the likeness and the lighting just right. Bird watchers and nature lovers will likewise wait quietly for countless hours, just to catch a glimpse of that special bird or animal. Fishing is another often solitary pursuit. Reading a book or a magazine or listening to a favourite piece of music are pastimes best enjoyed alone. This chapter looks at how we benefit from being alone.

## Why we need solitude

'Loneliness is the human condition. Cultivate it. The way it tunnels into you allows your soul room to grow,' says Janet Fitch in her novel *White Oleander* (Little, Brown, 1999). American philosopher Paul Tillich (1886–1965) said that language created the word 'loneliness' to express the pain of being alone, and the word 'solitude' to express the glory of being alone. Despite the bad press often given to loneliness, this is profoundly true. Often, people avoid being alone through fear of loneliness. But, as we've seen, other people aren't always the cure for loneliness. In addition, we all need emotional respite from the demands of others and a break from the stimulus of the outside world – if a baby is over-stimulated it 'tunes out' by turning its head away, closing its eyes, sneezing, crying or just going to sleep. We're not that different as adults. Indeed, our high need for sleep – given that we spend around a third of our lives snoozing – seems to indicate a profound natural need for some solitude for restoration and repair.

In our 24/7 world, with round-the-clock shopping, mobile phones and media, it can sometimes be easy to forget who we are and where we're going. Solitude provides space to think about this, and to develop and deepen a sense of purpose. It can also be an opportunity to slow down and experience life at a more natural pace. Human beings evolved over millions of years, and in all those millennia life was very much slower. The earth's population has doubled since the 1950s, and urban crowding and the new global economy have speeded up social relationships spectacularly, to the extent that we risk being 'terminally in touch', according to the *New York Times*. We also risk being out of touch – with ourselves. The need for constructive solitude can easily become lost, through today's fast-paced social interactions, or through panic that we are being excluded from these, or through simple fear of loneliness.

## But is it safe?

Traditionally, solitude has been accepted as a necessary environment for 'geniuses' such as artists and philosophers. 'A man can be himself only so long as he is alone . . . if he does not love solitude, he will not love freedom; for it is only when he is alone that he is really free,' says Schopenhauer in *The World as Will and Idea* (1818). Or take Voltaire: 'The happiest of all lives is a busy solitude.' This might be all right for lone geniuses and great writers, but psychologists have tended to be rather suspicious of solitude for the average person. Too much solitude was regarded as being bad for general well-being, with modern psychology focusing on the dangers of loneliness rather than the benefits of solitude. In the face of our cultural anxiety about isolation, psychiatrist Anthony Storr was one of the first to argue that solitude is necessary for mental health, creativity, fulfilment and emotional maturity. In his classic book *Solitude: A return to the self* (The Free Press, 1988), he posited that solitude provides space for the development of personality and that solitary pursuits 'play a greater part in the economy of human happiness than modern psycho-analysts and their followers allow'.

Since then, an emerging body of research – so-called 'solitude studies' – has been exploring the premise that solitude can be constructive, and that psychology's conventional approach to it – an 'almost exclusive emphasis on loneliness', according to Christopher Long of the University of Massachusetts – represented an artificially narrow view of what being alone entails. This research suggests that time alone is not only good for us but is essential for a variety of psychological processes. It can help us to recharge our batteries, to be clear about our focus, to have space for creative thinking. We may need to be alone simply to process emotional experiences. And, while it helps to chat through dilemmas with friends, problem-solving is another activity that is sometimes best done alone – solitude gives us the necessary space to work on problems and come up with creative solutions. This might be on an unconscious level or in a meditative state, for example while pottering in the garden, engaged in routine tasks or walking. Many of us have experienced that 'Aha!' moment while washing up or cleaning the car.

Harvard professor of psychology Daniel Gilbert, author of *Stumbling on Happiness* (Harper, 2006), led a study that suggests people form more lasting and accurate memories if they believe they're experiencing something individually and alone. Another Harvard study indicates that a certain amount of solitude can make a person more capable of empathy towards others. Some solitude, then, is essential for personal development.

## Solitude and inner strength

Cognitive transformation can be threatening rather than liberating. At the very least, in order to benefit from solitude, the individual must be able to draw on inner resources to find meaning in a situation in which external supports are lacking.

In their study 'Solitude: an exploration of benefits of being alone' (*Journal for the Theory of Social Behaviour* 33 (2003): 21–44), Christopher R. Long and James R. Averill of the University of Massachusetts have explored the way solitude can help strengthen resilience and inner strength. They define solitude as 'a state characterized by disengagement from the immediate demands of other people – a state of reduced social inhibition and increased freedom to select one's mental and physical activities'.

Throughout human history there have been people who preferred to live a solitary life in the country or as a hermit in a cave. The poet Emily Dickinson was renowned for her reclusive life, speaking to visitors from behind her bedroom door. In his book *In Search of the English Eccentric* (John Murray, 2008), author Henry Hemming explores along with other subjects the world of the recluse who refuses to live by society's conventions.

Solitude goes beyond the rather grudging phrase 'time out' with its implications of a snatched hour here and there as a kind of psychic paracetamol, a life-saver when the social pressures all get too much. For some, solitude, especially if habitual and practised with other disciplines such as meditation and prayer, may be transformative. Some people, such as monks and nuns, welcome long periods of solitude as a chance to develop self-reliance and inner strength, and to ponder and reflect at length on ideas and beliefs. Meditation and spirituality have been long associated with solitude. Some choose to live in closed orders, totally separate from the outside world. Art expert and author Sister Wendy Beckett chose a life of almost total solitude and contemplation, living in a caravan outside the Carmelite monastery where she has lived for over 40 years, only seeing the nun who looks after her once a day, communicating by note with the other nuns, and even refusing a pet. Her television appearances and books were undertaken to earn a living. Apart from looking after her health, this is the only reason she will break her life of solitude.

## Lonely or a loner?

Clinical psychologist Ros Taylor explains that a loner can be perfectly content in his or her own company. A natural loner finds it nourishing and sustaining to be alone for long periods. On the other hand, this will make most people feel very unhappy and lonely. It's all about finding the level that suits you. But even loners shouldn't cut themselves off completely from others, as we are still social creatures and we do need contact with others to feel well and content in the longer term. Problems are a possibility for loners who cut themselves off too much, believes Ros Taylor, as they can lose communication and social skills. A certain amount of interaction is necessary for us all.

## Extroverts and introverts

How much you need solitude is believed to be linked to how extrovert or introvert you are.

The terms 'introversion' and 'extroversion', popularized by Carl Jung, are basically a reflection of how much we need our energy to be fed by others and by the outside world.

*Extroverts* tend to get their energy from the outer world of people and objects, and feel drained and tired when they are by themselves too long.

*Introverts* are more likely to get their energy from their own inner world of ideas and images. Introverts are not necessarily shy or reclusive – indeed, they may be gregarious and enjoy company. However, they may only have limited energy for socializing, and tend to need solitude in order to recharge their batteries.

It may be helpful to think of extroversion and introversion being moods or phases that are both applicable to everyone at different times, reflecting a natural balance in our need for society and solitude. We all practise extroversion and introversion at different times and in different circumstances. Even those of us with high social tolerance benefit from time to ourselves, with solitude balancing and enriching our encounters with others.

However, some research indicates that our social needs go beyond psychology. Neuroscientists have identified physiological differences in the brains of extroverts and introverts. For example, researchers from the University of Iowa and the University of Texas showed that introverts experienced increased blood flow in the frontal lobes, the anterior thalamus and other structures associated with memory, planning and problem solving, whereas extroverts had more activity in the posterior thalamus and posterior insula, used to interpret sensory data. This suggests that it makes sense to gauge your individual need and tolerance for society.

## Measuring introversion and extroversion

The Myers-Briggs® Type Indicator (MBTI), based on Carl Jung's theories, measures introversion and extroversion, among other qualities.

### Extroversion

- I like getting my energy from active involvement in events and having a lot of different activities.
- I'm excited when I'm around people and I like to energize other people.
- I like moving into action and making things happen.
- I generally feel at home in the world.
- I often understand a problem better when I can talk out loud about it and hear what others have to say.
- I am seen as 'outgoing' or as a 'people person'.
- I feel comfortable in groups and like working in them.
- I have a wide range of friends and know lots of people.
- I sometimes jump too quickly into an activity and don't allow enough time to think it over.
- Before I start a project, I sometimes forget to stop and get clear on what I want to do and why.

### Introversion

- I like getting my energy from dealing with the ideas, pictures, memories and reactions that are inside my head, in my inner world.
- I often prefer doing things alone or with one or two people I feel comfortable with.
- I take time to reflect so that I have a clear idea of what I'll be doing when I decide to act. Ideas are almost solid things for me.
- Sometimes I like the idea of something better than the real thing.
- I am seen as 'reflective' or 'reserved'.
- I feel comfortable being alone and like things I can do on my own.
- I prefer to know just a few people well.
- I sometimes spend too much time reflecting and don't move into action quickly enough.

- I sometimes forget to check with the outside world to see if my ideas really fit the experience.

(Adapted from Charles R. Martin, *Looking at Type: The fundamentals*, Florida: CAPT, 1997)

## Who needs friends?

The answer is that we all do. But there are variations in the numbers of friends we need and the depth of that friendship, a sort of 'friendship quotient' if you like. Here's how you can work that out for yourself.

1 Think about your ideal social life. Take your time and try to imagine it for a few moments. How would your day begin? What kind of day would you have? Now follow numbers 2–8.
2 Would you prefer to have a partner? Score 10 for yes, 0 for no.
3 If so, how many hours of each day and night would you want to spend with your partner on average? Score between 1 and 24.
4 How close and intimate would you prefer to be with your partner? Score this between 1 and 10, 1 being the lowest and 10 being the highest level of intimacy.
5 How many close friends would suit you best? Score 2 points for each.
6 How close would you want close friends to be? Score your answer between 1 and 10, with 10 being the closest.
7 What about acquaintances? How many seems about right to you? Score yourself 1 for each.
8 Now add up your scores from questions 1–5 to give your 'friendship quotient'.
9 You can compare this to a notional maximum score of approximately 100, or with these scores:
   - *Person A*, who prefers to be single, with two or three close friends, and five or six acquaintances, would score 17.
   - *Person B*, who wants to spend most of each day with a very close and intimate partner, have ten very close friends and 30 acquaintances, would score 94.

Although you now have a measure of your ideal social life, the main reason for doing this is to gain a deeper understanding of what it is you are missing if you are feeling lonely. You may have a loving partner, but don't see him or her enough. You may have one very good close friend, but would really be more content with three or four.

## Women and solitude

Women are often programmed to put others' needs before their own, and as a result their needs for solitude can become confused. Clarissa Pinkola Estes is a Jungian analyst and storyteller, or *cantadora*, who has written about the healing aspects of solitude with a particular emphasis on women, especially those who feel obliged to be all things to all people. For example, she believes that much of a woman's pre-menstrual 'crankiness' is not just physical but is due to her 'being thwarted in her need to take enough time away to revivify and renew herself'. In her book *Women who Run with the Wolves* (Ballantine, 1992), she says that: 'if we establish a regular practice of intentional solitude, we invite a conversation between ourselves and the wild soul . . . the purpose of this union is for us to ask questions, and for the soul to advise.' She adds that: 'After a period of time, the cumulative effect of intentional solitude begins to act like a vital respiratory system, a natural rhythm of adding knowledge, making minute adjustments, and deleting the unusable over and over again.'

Perhaps the key phrase here is '*intentional* solitude'. It's generally agreed that, ideally, solitude is a free choice to spend time apart from people, rather than something we're forced into by circumstances or by others. This type of solitude can be a cure for that particularly painful type of loneliness that is shared with intimate or work relationships – that is, when the presence of other people results in increased loneliness, as discussed in Chapter 3.

## Solitary confinement

Some people have had solitude forced upon them, with their endurance a testament to their resilience in what is recognized as one of the harshest methods of punishment and torture. Helen Bamber, director of the Medical Foundation for the Care of Victims of Torture, says, 'Keeping someone in a state of isolation, with no means of renewing their intellectual life, has been described as killing a man without his dying.'

Well-known examples are Nelson Mandela, who spent 27 years in prison in South Africa; Terry Waite, the church envoy who was kept hostage in solitary confinement for almost five years in Beirut and released in 1991; and armed forces personnel who spent years living in POW camps during the First and Second World Wars. There are many inspirational stories of the amazing objects POWs made while incarcerated, sometimes from the most meagre and humble resources. To relieve the boredom and loneliness, they could make objects such as board games, chess sets, straw hats and models of ships. To be alone is never the end. Woo Yong-gak, political prisoner in South Korea who was released in 1999 after 41 years of solitary confinement, says, 'I endured it with a strong will.'

## Solitude and teenagers

While the best solitude is voluntary, some research suggests it can also act as a tonic even when time alone isn't altogether a pleasant experience. Research by Dr Reed Larson of the University of Illinois suggests that teenagers may need solitude to help develop their notoriously volatile sense of self – as well as to improve their moods and achieve good grades in school. Conversely, it appears that adolescents unable to cope with being alone are less likely to develop their creative abilities. For teenagers, as for the rest of us, some loneliness may simply be the price of forging a clearer identity.

The teenagers in Larson's study weren't necessarily happier when they were alone – after all, peer pressure is a large part of what being a teenager is all about. But Larson found that doses of solitude acted like a 'bitter medicine' – the adolescents' mental and emotional health improved after they spent some time alone. So how much of the medicine should you take? Unfortunately, the bottle doesn't come with instructions. While solitude may be good for your psychological health, individuals have to work out the right dose for themselves.

## Summary

- Being on your own provides respite from the demands of others, and allows you to experience a slower and more natural pace of life.
- Some people welcome solitude for creative and spiritual purposes, and for personal development.
- People have to work out their own comfortable level for solitude. We all have a different loneliness threshold.

# 6

# Bereavement

The loneliness of bereavement is something many of us can identify with all too easily. We tend to use the term 'bereaved' only when a person very close to us has died, meaning the loss is a significant one, with a huge impact. We have lost a parent, child, partner or other loved one. This loneliness may not be felt straight away. The hard truth is that there's so much to be done after a death. With so much to organize and sort out, arrangements to be made and people around most of the time, there is rarely a moment on your own to begin to think about what it all means and to try to get your head round what has happened. And there is probably still the numbness that protects us from the enormity of the loss – until we have time enough to take it in.

Losing a loved one is the most stressful experience we can have. It is very similar to an acute stress reaction – it has in fact been compared to post-traumatic stress reaction, such as that experienced after war, natural disaster, a road accident or an assault. This is particularly so if death is sudden, such as a car crash or a heart attack or stroke, coming completely out of the blue and bringing you abruptly face to face with a tremendous loss. And even though many deaths come after a long illness such as cancer, the impact of the actual ending is still not to be under-estimated. Either way, bereavement is a massive shock.

There is no 'right' way or 'wrong' way to grieve. There is no 'normal' way to react to a death. Everyone experiences it differently, and learns a new way of living in their own way and in their own time. Grief can take many forms, and Table 6.1 shows just some of the many and varied but quite normal reactions and experiences which a bereaved person may have in the days and weeks immediately following the loss.

In the days and weeks after the funeral, some bereaved people immerse themselves in work or daily tasks, while others find the

**Table 6.1 Some of the ways we can respond to grief**

| Feelings | Normal grief reactions | | Behaviour |
| --- | --- | --- | --- |
| | Physical sensations | Thinking | |
| • Loneliness | • Tightness in chest | • Preoccupation | • Disturbed |
| • Fatigue | or throat | with thoughts | sleep |
| • Sadness | • Hollowness in | about | • Appetite |
| • Anger | chest or stomach | deceased | disturbed |
| • Guilt | • Oversensitive to | • Disbelief | • Social |
| • Anxiety | noise | • Confusion | withdrawal |
| • Helplessness | • Feeling of | • Sense of | • Restless |
| • Shock | unreality | presence | overactivity |
| • Yearning or | • Weakness in | • Hearing or | • Crying/not |
| pining | muscles | seeing the | crying |
| • Numbness | • Lack of energy | deceased (this | |
| | • Sighing | is normal) | |

simplest of activities beyond them and lose all sense of a routine. It's also common to face your own mortality and to start thinking about your own death, perhaps for the first time, and this can be a tremendously isolated place suddenly to find yourself.

In the weeks and months following a death, it is understandable if you withdraw, not meeting friends, avoiding going to the gym or that art class you had been enjoying. Life has changed profoundly, and the usual day-to-day activities may seem very remote. You can find yourself avoiding the neighbours as you don't know what to say and don't want to have to talk about it, and they do the same with you. As a result, you may find yourself cut off from your old comfortable social life, and invitations gradually dwindle because you keep making excuses when a friend suggests an outing to the cinema or for a drink. Before you know it, you can feel isolated and alone.

## How long will it last?

I've heard people saying things like, 'She should be over it by now, that's six months', about someone who has recently lost her partner of 20 years or more. And this is just nonsense. Adjusting to bereavement takes much longer than that, and maybe you haven't even started to come to terms with what has happened. Your life is still completely up in the air. The house is so empty all of a sudden.

Grief is not something you 'get over', it's something you adapt to. Life will never be the same again. But in time a new way of life and being begins to fit into place, which takes you forward again. How long grief lasts very much varies from person to person, and there are absolutely no hard and fast rules. It's often said, though, that grief lasts longer than you expect it to last. It sometimes helps to think of bereavement as a process which can progress gradually through stages. This is very much a generalization, and many people will only go through one or two stages or may not follow this process at all. But models like these can sometimes help us to understand grief a little better, and also make it easier to recognize when someone's grief is getting out of hand.

One example of the stages of grief is described by J. William Worden, and I've found this model particularly helpful myself. Distressing though grieving most certainly is, he puts forward the idea that grief actually serves a useful function, and that it is made up of four 'tasks', coming one after the other in a fixed order. These four tasks he describes as:

1 Task 1: to accept the reality of the loss.
2 Task 2: to work your way through the grief and the pain which goes with it.
3 Task 3: to adjust to a world without the person who has died.
4 Task 4: to 'emotionally relocate' the person you've lost, and move on with life.

The first three tasks are self-explanatory, but perhaps the fourth is less clear. When, as a bereaved person, you *emotionally relocate* the person you have lost, you find a place for that person in your emotional life which will allow you to continue effectively with your life and relationships. The person will be relocated from an active relationship into a new emotional setting, and a new kind of relationship. So a widow may eventually find that she remembers her husband especially at times when there are choices to be made for the family, and she may think: what would he have done or advised? A mother will remember her lost son and chat to him briefly every morning when she sees his picture on the mantel. A husband has a folder of precious photographs of his wife, which he looks through every evening, and tells her the news. But at the same time, each of these bereaved people can also begin to get on with life and even form new relationships.

## Mourning

Worden also talks about how long grief lasts and how it affects people's feelings, thoughts and behaviour. There is a very real sense in which mourning is never over, as you can miss the presence of a loved one for your entire life. I certainly do.

But here are some other general thoughts on how long it might last:

- It may last until Tasks 1–4 are finished.
- It's unlikely to be less than one year, and two is not unlikely.
- A benchmark may be when you are able to think of the lost person without pain.
- Studies show that fewer than half of women who lose their husband are 'themselves' again at the end of a year, but that at around two years the majority have found some sort of new stability.

Death is still one of our society's taboos. People don't like to talk about it and don't really know what to say to a bereaved person. Over the last 100 years, medicine has made massive advances, with numerous immunizations becoming readily available for killer illnesses such as typhoid, polio, diphtheria and smallpox. Penicillin and a host of other antibiotics were discovered, and treatments developed for common diseases such as tuberculosis and diabetes, which previously were fatal. Childbirth has become a much safer process for women, at least in developed countries like the UK. Before this multitude of life-saving developments, death was an everyday reality for most people. Many children died in infancy or never reached adulthood, and the many infectious diseases of the time took many people's lives long before they retired. People could talk about death more easily then, and mourning was marked for long periods by wearing dark clothing. In the house where someone had died, curtains remained closed until the funeral was over, or sometimes longer.

Nowadays, when death often takes place out of sight and has become more taboo, we often just don't know what to say to someone who has had a close bereavement. I remember when a neighbour of mine that I'd known fairly well for a number of years lost her husband suddenly from a heart attack at the age of 45. About six weeks later I met her at the bus stop. We exchanged pleasantries about the weather and chatted about what time the next bus was likely to appear, and she seemed comfortable with that. It would have been easy for me just to continue in that vein and to take the easy way out by not mentioning her loss. But that just seemed so wrong. So I said to her that I was so sorry to hear that her husband had died, and that she must miss him terribly. She looked slightly taken aback, and didn't answer straight away. For a moment I thought I'd done the wrong thing, but a look of gratitude and emotion suddenly came across her face, and she said, 'You know I'm so glad you said that. I really do appreciate it. Most people just go on as if nothing's happened and I should be over it by now. That makes me feel terrible. It's all still so raw. And yes, I do miss him so much.' We then went on to talk about what had happened the day he died, and how difficult it had become for her even to come out of the house and do a bit of shopping. She looked relieved to just talk normally about what had become her new reality.

Here are some things you can do when grieving, which may ease the pain a little and help you to maintain your social network as much as possible:

- Help yourself to make the loss more real – by talking about it, talking about the person and using his or her name.
- Look for opportunities to express your feelings.
- Accept offers of practical help for things like getting the bills paid, doing the shopping, mowing the lawn or clearing out possessions.
- Give yourself time to grieve, and be aware that it can be especially difficult at certain times – for example, three months after the death, at holidays, Christmas, birthdays, anniversaries, and so on.

- Don't expect everyone to be the same as you – people grieve in different ways and for different lengths of time.
- Accept any continuing support you are offered, especially at critical periods, for at least the first year.
- Try not to let the things people say and do upset you too much. People mean well but are just not good at knowing how to go about this: 'I know how you feel' (when you know they couldn't possibly), 'Be brave', and platitudes such as 'Life is for the living' or 'Time is a great healer'. Friends and neighbours often feel helpless, so you could acknowledge this by saying something like, 'I don't know what to say to you. I'm sure you don't know what to say to me.'
- Writing a letter to the loved one, expressing your thoughts and feelings, can be an uplifting experience. This helps take care of unfinished business and things you need to say, but it may take some time before you are able to cope with this.
- If you're scared you'll forget the person who has died – how someone looked, the sound of a beloved voice, the good times you had together – keep your memories alive by talking about him or her and your special memories, or write down these memories and make up a special photograph album, or a box with the loved one's special possessions. You could even commemorate someone's life by paying for a park bench with a plaque or by planting a tree.

## Make sure to keep your friends

When you are grieving it is extremely easy to lose touch with friends and family, as well as acquaintances, and neighbours. They feel awkward, and so do you. And just keeping up with all these people and relationships is just a mountain too far for you. But remember, it's possible and it's acceptable to grieve and live at the same time. Your grief won't pass in a week or two, so for some considerable time it will be your companion as you live your life.

There will be ups and downs, and good days and bad days, and there will sometimes be that familiar fragrance, or a certain piece of music, or you'll see someone who looks like your loved one, and suddenly the grief can return as painfully as ever as you hold back the tears in the shopping mall or at the office. When my mother died a few years ago, it was a long time before I could smile or laugh without feeling guilty, or even enjoy a good meal. But we have to do these things. We are alive, and we have a life to live. We owe it to our lost loved ones to make the most of what they no longer have. So, despite such feelings, after a bit of time has passed and when you feel ready, it's perfectly all right to accept offers to go out with friends for a quiet drink or a lunch, or go to a show or to see a band. Don't turn friends away who want to help – maybe say you're not ready yet but ask them to please ask again soon.

If friends want to visit, let them – they may well be anxious about knowing the right things to say, so let them know that there's nothing they can say or need to say: just being there with you is enough. Explain that nothing can take away the hurt, but having someone beside you feels better than being alone. If it helps you to talk about your loved one, tell this to your friends; likewise if you prefer not to.

If you have already let friendships drift because of grief, it's never too late to pick things up again. Don't try to do everything at once, just try one small step, whatever you can manage. Try a text or a quick e-mail or phone call just asking, 'How are you?' People will understand why you've not been in touch, and will respond. If they don't get back to you, don't assume they don't want to – they may be having problems themselves. If you want to rejoin a group of some kind, just go along to the next meeting, and you'll be welcomed back. Or phone someone you got on well with at the group, and go along with him or her if that helps. A warm smile if you see your neighbour or an acquaintance, even if you haven't spoken in a while, can break even the thickest of ice.

## When to seek help

If the grief and loneliness are becoming too much to bear, or your grief feels as if it's been going on for too long, or maybe you feel you are becoming depressed, it's best to seek help from your doctor or a specialist group or counsellor. There is much that these people can do to help you, and they will understand what you're going through better than you think.

## Summary

- A close bereavement is one of the most stressful experiences you can have.
- The question 'How long should mourning last?' is difficult to answer, but it can be said that mourning is never really over.
- It can be easy when you're grieving to let friendships and outside interests slip.
- There are things you can do when you're grieving to ease the pain a little, and help you to keep in touch with friends and family.
- If grief and loneliness become too much for you to bear, or you feel it's all going on too long, talk things over with a trusted friend or family member, or with your doctor.

# 7

## Friendships that last

We already know that meaningful and satisfying relationships are an integral part of what makes us human. Feeling connected to a group and feeling responsibility for others entails a deeper sense of purpose and meaning, which makes for a happier life. Relationships with friends and partners can protect and support us in difficult times, and make us emotionally strong and resilient. One study asked people to rate the gradient of a hill and to estimate how difficult it would be to climb. In the presence of a friend, people saw the slope as less steep. And the closer the friend, the easier the climb appeared. This feeling of belonging also means we're more likely to take care of ourselves and take fewer risks, which in turn translates into better long-term health. However, many of us lack these vital sources of support. And we can lose confidence and get out of practice at socializing. But so can other people. You're not the only one. There are loads of other lonely people out there just waiting to be met.

The key is action. This doesn't mean you have to turn into a social butterfly or party animal overnight, but just to accommodate a slight shift in attitude that will allow you to be more pro-active in socializing.

The reality is that building up your social network will probably mean you have to make the first move. New friends may be met in all sorts of unexpected places, but you may not be able to rely on people coming to you.

### The friendship effect

One study by Cacioppo suggests that loneliness may be contagious. In a ten-year study, researchers examined how loneliness spreads in social networks. The results indicated that people close to someone experiencing loneliness were 52 per cent more likely to become

lonely as well. Conversely, the happiness of our friends is infectious, according to researchers at Harvard and the University of
California. In a study that measured the happiness of nearly 5,000
individuals over a period of 20 years, reports showed that when an
individual was happy it spread through that person's network of
friends, and on through the friends' friends, and the measurable
effect could last for up to a year.

A raft of studies has proved what we've always known – a good
social network is very important to our well-being and health.
Just how important, though, is highlighted by the sometimes
startling results of the studies listed below. Some studies show
that, for women in particular, friendship is vital, especially in
times of stress – although equally it's often the first thing to go
when a woman is pressured for time because of work and family
commitments.

- The long-running Nurses' Health Studies from Harvard Medical
  School found that not having close friends or confidants was
  as bad for your health as smoking or carrying extra weight.
  Conversely, the more friends women have, the less likely they
  are to develop physical impairments as they age, and the more
  likely they are to be happy to be leading a full and happy life.
  The researchers also found that women with a close friend and
  confidant survived the death of their partner much better than
  their solitary counterparts, in terms of both emotional and
  physical health.
- Similar findings were reported by researchers from Brigham
  Young University, who analysed nearly 150 studies to conclude
  that having few friends is as damaging to survival as smoking
  15 cigarettes a day or being alcoholic. Losing social support was
  shown to cut the odds of survival far more than being obese
  or not exercising. In their study, which looked at over 300,000
  people from four continents over seven years, those with the
  strongest social networks were 1.5 times as likely to be alive at
  any given age than those who were lonely. A good network of
  friends and neighbours boosts survival chances by 50 per cent.
- And an Australian team of scientists found that having friends
  around in old age can do more for life expectancy than having

family members around. The team analysed social, health and lifestyle data of more than 1,500 people over 70 from the Australian Longitudinal Study of Aging (ALSA), which began in 1992 in Adelaide, South Australia.

## Learning social skills

Can social skills be taught? Yes, it would seem, and to a very wide range of people, from international high-fliers to those with social difficulties.

Although finishing schools are now largely defunct, the traditional Institut Villa Pierrefeu remains open in Switzerland and still teaches (at huge expense) international etiquette, protocol and *savoir-vivre*, among other subjects. The rather newer Finishing Academy, in Cheshire, teaches etiquette to women and men along with a range of other life skills from how to sew on a button (for the older widowed gentleman) to how to carve a joint, choose hobbies, master first aid and even maintain a car. E-mail etiquette, self-defence and deportment – or its modern version, body language – also feature. On-line courses are available too. High Society Secrets, one of a London-based range of establishments, also teaches poise and the art of social sophistication, and other skills that often blend into the realm of personal development, itself a multi-billion pound industry.

The link between social and personal development is poignantly illustrated by a study at the University of California, Los Angeles (UCLA), which showed that teenagers with high-functioning autism benefited significantly from classes in social etiquette. Hard as life is for teenagers in general, it's even harder for those with autism spectrum disorders (ASD) as they typically lack perception of basic social cues such as body language and facial expressions, and speech inflections like warmth or sarcasm. Sadly, long-lasting isolation can be the result.

Clinical instructor of psychiatry Elizabeth Laugeson and colleagues developed the class, called PEERS (Program for the Education and Enrichment of Relational Skills), to teach a range of specific social skills, including:

- how to comfortably join and exit a group of peers;
- how to pick the right peer group;
- practising good sportsmanship;
- being a good host;

- how to change a bad reputation;
- handling teasing, bullying and arguments.

In line with the needs of teens with autism, who tend to learn by rote, the class was highly structured, with the skills broken down into small steps. If teased, for example, they might be taught the classic teenager's comeback: 'Whatever!' By the end of the classes, the teenagers were much more socially confident and had more social interactions.

So even rote-learned social skills serve a vital purpose, with the evidence indicating that others respond to them as if they were genuine.

## Friendship skills

Good social skills are also good friendship skills, and they grow and develop with you. So, while it may seem a little artificial to think in terms of consciously honing friendship skills, working at relationships does pay off. Here are 12 friendship skills to be aware of:

- Ability to share possessions and space
- Keeping confidences and secrets
- Offering to help
- Accepting others' mistakes
- Being positive and enthusiastic
- Starting a conversation
- Winning and losing well
- Listening to others
- Starting and maintaining a conversation
- Ignoring someone who is annoying you
- Co-operating with others
- Giving and receiving compliments.

One of the best ways to nurture a friendship and cement long-lasting relationships is to be a good friend yourself. Look for unobtrusive ways to build friendships, such as listening, bringing a small gift, or being the first one to make the call or send the e-mail. And give it time. Some friendships are instantaneous, others may take months and years to develop.

## First, nurture your friends

Finding new people is a vital part of our social growth and expansion, but it's so important to nurture your existing friendships too. This may be especially important for women, who often let friendships drift for the sake of work and family. Professor of clinical psychology Ruthellen Josselson, co-author of *Best Friends: The pleasures and perils of girls' and women's friendships* (Three Rivers Press, 1998), says that unpressured time for friendships is vital and healing for women.

So the first and easiest thing you can do is pick up on relationships you already have with friends or family, and begin to get more involved with these again. Call that friend you're always meaning to call, and if you're asked to join some of the family for lunch or a day out then say yes this time. Ask them back to yours for a coffee afterwards.

As we've seen, it's becoming less common to keep in touch with childhood and school friends. Life is busy for everyone, and it's very common for friends to drift apart or lose touch these days, because of moves, job changes and divorce and separation, leaving friendship networks in a constant state of flux and change. One in three women say they have already lost at least 26 friends by the time they reach the age of 30 – a staggering average of one a year since starting primary school, according to a report by the internet site Friends Reunited. But getting back in touch after a long time is also much more common than you might think. Sites such as Friends Reunited, which has nine million registered members, have become a massive success for this very reason. So do seek out the lost people in your life. Even if it's been a while, old friends are usually keen to pick up where you left off.

## Why people fall out

Here are the top five reasons why friends fall out, according to a survey of 2,636 members of Friends Reunited as part of an ongoing investigation by their Friendship Panel:

- Lives moving on – the main reason
- All take and no give

- Misjudged character
- Infidelity
- Jealousy.

## Shared interests

Some experts believe that shared interests and tasks form more of a foundation for male friendships than for female ones, with women perceived to be more unconditional in their friendships. From the viewpoint of evolutionary psychology, this may be rooted in 'reciprocal altruism' – traditionally, men shared hunter-gatherer tasks for the good of the community and in the interests of common survival. Charles Darwin himself considered the adaptive advantage of sympathy in *The Descent of Man*, though it troubled him that it stemmed from a 'low motive', i.e. survival. This kind of thinking, as with other evolutionary psychology explanations, has been criticized as assuming rather too much of evolution. Palaeontologist and science writer Stephen Jay Gould and biologist Richard Lewontin have suggested that certain traits might simply be by-products of evolution rather than the direct results of evolution and adaption – 'spandrels', as they put it.

You might agree that the best friendships move on – or up – from this rather utilitarian view of friendship, and that we choose our friends because of what they are, not what they can give. In the words of Anaïs Nin, 'Each friend represents a world in us, a world possibly not born until they arrive, and it is only by this meeting that a new world is born.'

Others might argue that perceived differences in male and female friendships are outdated in any case.

Certainly, research has pinpointed shared interests and community activities as a vital way of maintaining a sense of purpose and counteracting feelings of futility. Professor Timothy Wilson, professor of psychology at the University of Virginia and author of *REDIRECT: The surprising new science of psychological change* (Allen Lane, 2011), says that for most of us caring for our families is the primary goal, but that we need to consider a sense of purpose when choosing careers and hobbies as well.

So, when thinking about activities and interests you enjoy or want to try, from keeping fit to campaigning, consider how much they contribute to your sense of purpose. That way not only will you be connecting with people with similar interests, but you'll also be feeding your own sense of meaning in life.

However, you don't have to spend hours choosing the right activity. Just choose something which is of reasonable interest to you, and go for it. It doesn't have to be the absolutely right one – it's still getting the social muscles going. Don't expect everything to fall into place in a week or two. Give it time, and if it doesn't work quite as expected you can always move on.

## EASE

*Loneliness: Human nature and the need for social connection* suggests four simple steps, in the acronym 'EASE':

### E is for Extend Yourself

It is important to extend yourself, but do this in small ways. Loneliness tends to result in withdrawal and passivity, and when you're out of the habit of socializing, reaching out to others can feel disproportionately threatening. So create new social habits slowly, and little by little. 'Don't focus on trying to find the love of your life or to reinvent yourself all at once. Just slip a toe in the water.' The aim is to start experiencing small amounts of more positive social interaction. Volunteer work can be a safer environment in which to break the cycle of social fear and start building social confidence.

### A is for Action Plan

Feelings of passivity tend to go hand in hand with feelings of loneliness. However, we have more control than we sometimes think. We can choose where to invest our social energy, and that change doesn't have to be enormous. Be alert for social cues, but bear in mind these may include cues that suggest caution. Don't commit to too many things or people in an effort to prove you can beat loneliness. Just be realistically open to engagement – in other words, be human!

## S is for Selection

The solution to loneliness is not quantity but quality of relationships, which need to be meaningful and satisfying. Look for compatible people, who share common beliefs and interests, rather than being attracted by physical appearance or status.

## E is for Expect the Best

A positive, warm outlook is more likely to elicit a warm, positive response. Give it time and patience, and don't expect perfection even when you do start to feel happier and less lonely. There's a reason why wedding vows are 'for better or for worse', says Cacioppo. 'Even the best friends and the partners in the best marriages will disagree and hurt each other from time to time.'

## Making new friends

Think about your skills, talents and interests. Make a list of them. Try and be honest about your strengths and limitations. For example, Christine's list looked like this:

- Background in arts PR and arts magazines
- Creative – love making the home look arty and cosy
- Interest in health stemming from my own poor health (migraine and ME)
- Good empathy, good listener – interested in others and in local events
- Don't have much tolerance for time-wasting committees and meetings – need a healthy dose of solitude
- Time and energy limited by caring role (looking after elderly mother)
- Good at juggling but tend to take too much on, so can be disorganized.

After considering her options, Christine decided to:

- write for a local magazine, especially about any arty activities or people in the area;
- help organize the local jazz festival, but on her own terms and as

far as possible without getting involved with the committee and the irritating local disagreements;

- pay someone to come in three afternoons a week to visit her mother, to give her more time for her own life.

However, she decided to drop her on-line involvement with an ME group as she found it time-consuming and unproductive, and also not to respond to the frequent requests from local organizations for free PR work and tips, as although they assuaged her loneliness at first they soon ended up wasting her talents and time. Instead, she's considering setting up her own web page as a PR consultant.

Is there something there you could get involved with? Could you do a refresher course on a skill you have, or learn more about it? Do you have a skill you could use to help others, through a local charity? If you don't like small talk, joining in with an interest group helps to avoid most of that, as they tend to go straight into talking about the activity they're involved with. A photographic club, an aerobics class or a local history group are typical examples. Leisure pursuits and interests like running, cycling, amateur dramatics, dancing, singing or martial arts – in fact, anything which involves using your voice or your body confidently (or preferably both) – are particularly good at improving your confidence in yourself, even without the added social benefits. Information about what's available in your area can be found in the local press, local libraries and community centres, on the internet, and so on.

Voluntary work comes up repeatedly in studies as a relatively safe launching pad for social activities. It involves far less risk of rejection. It's also more likely to give you a sense of achievement and the valuable feeling of having helped someone or an important cause, so building self-worth. There is a huge range available, with something to suit everyone – working with animals, volunteering at a homeless shelter, teaching computer skills to older people, volunteer taxi-driving for hospital patients, helping with children's sport – the list is endless. But, as with any other social activity, it pays to be discriminating. There's no point getting involved in the local am-dram as a would-be leading lady if you get stage fright – though they might be delighted to have your talents as wardrobe mistress or treasurer.

Other ideas of how to get out there and meet people include:

- Campaigning group – again, there is tremendous choice, and the chance to feel you're doing something.
- Community group – it's easy to get chatting if you're planting bulbs or picking up litter in the local park.
- Church or other religious grouping – most have a wide variety of activities.
- Work social events – give one a try.
- Take an activity or special interest holiday or weekend break – they're very popular these days, and many go alone.
- Take a course – anything will do: learn a language, learn to cook or use a computer.
- Join a special interest group or club – all kinds: writing, gardening, yoga, book club, meditation, photography, crafts, and so on.
- Get yourself a dog – daily walks are proven to be good for your emotional and physical health, and dogs draw conversation from other people like a magnet, so you're much more likely to meet people than when walking alone. Incidentally, don't overlook venues like the shops and supermarkets – a surprising number of people have met in this way.
- Sport – doing or watching, or a session at the gym or a fitness class. Exercise will also make you feel more content, and help you lose weight and tone up if you want to.
- Dancing – all sorts to choose from.
- Local walkers or jogging groups – lots of these for all abilities; check the local press or the internet. Many go alone to these too.

A few points to remember:

- New friends are unlikely to appear at your door, so you need to get out there and meet new people.
- Nurture your existing friendships, and any new ones you form. Only make friends with positive people who can give and take.
- Look for new friendships based on shared interests.

# 8

# Brush up your social skills

All relationships tend to make use of habits and customs called social skills – a smile, a nod, exchanging a few words, handshakes, air kisses, small talk, and so on. This chapter looks at the mechanics of how we socialize.

Let's begin with one of the most basic parts of socializing, making conversation. For many people, this all seems to come perfectly naturally, making it all the worse for those who find that it's not so easy and can be quite daunting for one reason or another. There are many reasons for finding that socializing doesn't come easily and this can cause considerable anxiety for many people. As babies we come pre-programmed to interact with others. In fact, a baby's large eyes and cute gurgling and cooing are designed to be attractive to adult humans, ensuring that the baby receives lots of attention. Early baby talk is the start of socializing and learning how to take turns and communicate with other people. Let's look a bit more at the art of conversation and how you can easily become better at it. The focus will mainly be on conversation between two people, but everything said will apply just as much in small groups of people.

## Turn-taking

There are two parts to a conversation: talking and listening. In a good conversation, we take turns to speak and to listen. As already said, we learn this skill from very early on, as babies.

Imagine if, when two people are talking, the person who is speaking holds a ball, then passes it to the other person when it's that person's turn to speak. In an everyday conversation, each person should have the ball for about an equal amount of the time, with the ball passing back and forth a bit like a good, long tennis rally. Here is a short extract from an everyday conversation between two people, Jack and Jane:

*Jack:* How are you?
*Jane:* I'm good, thanks, how are you?
*Jack:* OK, thanks. What a great day this is.
*Jane:* Yes, fantastic weather, isn't it?
*Jack:* You got plans for today?
*Jane:* Yes. Headed into town.
*Jack:* Me too. Going in later.
*Jane:* You meeting up with someone in town?

Do you see the rhythm to the conversation, with 'turns' being taken in a roughly even pattern? Each person responds to what the other has just said, and leads the conversation on a little further, along a logical road. If one person hogs the talking, he or she will be seen as selfish or boring.

## Better listening

Listening is not the entirely passive experience you may imagine it to be. Good listening is *active* listening. It's about actually hearing what is said and understanding it, and showing that you've heard and understood. It's about knowing when to ask a question, and then taking time to listen to and understand the answer. Good listening is not a one-way street. It's a two-way street. It's about two people interacting with one another.

So listening is an active process. Problems can arise if you are too concerned about what you are saying, and concentrate too much on the impression you are making. You then have no time to actually listen to what the other person is saying. But it all becomes much easier if you can simply relax, go with the rhythm and the flow, forget yourself and get genuinely interested in the other person. Other people can be really interesting, if you just listen to them.

So the key thing to do if you want to improve your conversation skills is not to learn to be a better talker, it's to learn to become a better listener. Here are some suggestions for doing just that.

- Let the other person share the talking and listening equally (remember holding and passing the ball).
- Focus on the other person, not yourself.
- Really listen and pay attention.
- Actively engage with what is being said.

- Allow yourself to become genuinely interested in what's being said. Be interested and interesting.
- Notice the other person's body language – what is it telling you?
- Hear the emotion in what's being said, not just the words.
- Use facial expression and body language to show that you've understood, or are surprised, or amused or whatever.
- You don't have to come up with clever things to say – just listen to other people, and reflect back what they're saying, or ask them a question about themselves. People love that, and will like you for it.
- Look around you. Take your thoughts out from inside your head and look around you at other people, and what's going on with them, and at where you are.
- Learn to relax. If you're stressed, angry or upset, relaxing your body will calm the situation and your thinking, and will help you to cope better and focus better on what's being said. Try taking in a deep breath, and just letting all the tension go from your body as you breathe out. Repeat if necessary. More on how to relax and cope with stress in Chapter 11.

## Talking

As already said, if you can listen actively, you will find it much easier when it's your turn to say something. Here are some other thoughts which may be useful. Take this one step at a time, and don't try to do too much at once.

### Be yourself

Don't try to put on an act of any kind. All we're trying to do here is brush up on your skills, not make you into somebody else. It is impossible to maintain any kind of front, and being found out will undermine your confidence. Anyway, being a little shy can be quite attractive and may bring out the protective instinct in others. Have a practice at talking about yourself if you're out of the habit of it or find it daunting. This may sound a bit of a strange thing to do, but it's not really. We would be surprised if an athlete didn't practise or train before an event, or a musician hadn't practised with his or her guitar before playing for an audience. A pet is ideal for this, as you can easily chat away to it. There's no need to use a mirror unless that makes it easier. Try it when you're doing the washing up, or in the bath or shower, or just where it feels most comfortable. Imagine questions you might be asked, and work out simple straightforward answers.

## Use people's names

People you already know like you to use their name. They find this warm, supportive and encouraging. Don't worry if you don't remember everyone's names after one of those 'let me introduce you to everybody' moments. No-one does. If you're talking to someone later on, just say that you're sorry but you didn't catch everyone's names when you were introduced, and ask, 'Would you mind telling me your name again?' Most people understand this completely, as we've all been in that position.

## Use open questions and statements

Closed questions can be answered with a 'yes' or 'no', or a few words. Did you see your friend yesterday? Where do you live? What age are you? These can make a conversation stilted and more of an interrogation. So choose your questions with a bit of thought. Maybe plan a few questions in advance. Aim to use open questions, or open statements, which take a few sentences or more to answer. This adds depth to the conversation, and allows a usually welcome opening for someone to relate a story or some other experience. It gives others the opportunity to talk. People like that!

Open questions or statements will usually begin with words such as:

- How . . .
- Why . . .
- Tell me about . . .
- Describe . . .
- In what way . . .
- What about . . .
- How do you feel about . . .

A useful exercise:

1 Try making up a list of open questions and open statements that you might use in the kinds of conversation you are likely to be

involved in. Use the list of opening words just given as a starting point.

2 Try to make up at least one question for each opening word or phrase.

## Reflect

Reflecting back what you've just been told is a very powerful way to show you are listening with interest. It is also likely to encourage someone to go on and tell you more. If someone has just related to you all about his car problems over the past week, you might say, 'You've had it really bad this past week. You must be feeling annoyed about that.' He may well respond, 'You bet I do. It never seems to end. Just when I thought it was fixed. With my last car, it was all very different, I . . .'

## Give feedback on strengths

If someone relates to you an experience in which she has shown a strength of some kind, it is very helpful to tell her about that strength: 'You were very brave doing that', 'You showed such kindness there.' This can be very effective and help to build a relationship with that person.

Here's a summary so far, along with a few more ideas to have a think about:

- Don't feel you have to talk too much, or that the onus is on you to keep the conversation going. Just take your turn, as everyone else does.
- Be genuine – be yourself.
- Wait for a natural pause before you speak.
- Try not to interrupt the speaker.
- Use the person's name when appropriate.
- React to what the person is saying.
- Have an open mind.
- Use open questions or statements.
- Reflect back what's been said.
- Ask for more information.
- Give positive feedback on what's been said.
- Nod occasionally.

- Say 'uh-huh' or 'mm-hmm'.
- Avoid giving unwanted advice.
- Don't complain too much about your own problems.
- Avoid expressing very fixed or dogmatic views.

## Making small talk

Inevitably, on social occasions we are required to engage in 'small talk'. This can sometimes be difficult. The best advice here is simply to follow all the suggestions covered already in this chapter, including whenever possible remembering some background information on those you'll be talking to. You may find small talk boring – many people do – but unfortunately this is what socializing is often about, and it's how almost all meaningful relationships begin.

For people you already know, small talk at a social event usually begins with simple 'how are you?' sorts of questions, moving on to asking how someone's partner or family are. These sorts of questions will usually be reciprocated and asked of you, so have some basic information ready to give about this. Just talk about the basics: no need to go into great detail. I knew someone once who every time he was asked, 'How are you?' would go into immense detail about his state of health, hospital appointments, various medications and all sorts of stuff like that, droning on for at least ten minutes, and then would announce he had to get on and would disappear without so much as a reciprocal 'And how are you?' This is what's called 'too much information' and is to be avoided.

For people you've never met, conversation is more likely to begin with introductions, then move to comments about the event you're attending and how you got there, then to simple general discussion of where you're from, whether you work and if so at what, and so on. People like to get a thumbnail sketch of someone before moving forward with small talk. No point in asking someone who's been unemployed for three years where he or she went on holiday that summer. Skills we've learnt so far will see you safely through this stage. And the more practice you get, the better you'll be at this.

The best advice for small talk is to come prepared. So keep a bit of an eye on the news and current affairs, even if you don't usually. Buy a popular newspaper or magazine regularly to keep up with what's in and what's not. Watch a few of the most popular TV programmes for your age group, just to keep in touch. It's all worth the effort. Having a few thoughts and ideas ready on a range of everyday and non-controversial topics will never go wrong. It's always best to steer clear of potentially controversial subjects, at least until you build up your confidence.

Sometimes the reason small talk is difficult, especially after the first stages of a conversation, is because you actually don't have much to say. It's just that the topics which small talk centres around are not always of interest to everyone. Or you might be the kind of person who doesn't pay much attention to the stuff of small talk – what's in the news, community events, holidays, popular TV programmes, fashion trends, sport and so on. If you are from a younger or older age group, the topics discussed may be a bit different, but the advice is still the same.

## What to talk about

Here is a list of topics suitable for general small talk with a group of other people:

| | |
|---|---|
| The weather! | Pets |
| Sport | Food |
| Television programmes | Cooking |
| The news | Shops |
| Holidays | Shopping |
| Children | Driving |
| Parents | Music |
| Cars | Hobbies. |

- What do you know about each of these topics?
- For those you don't know anything about, how would you find out about them? This doesn't need to be much, just enough to take part in a low-key conversation.
- Think out what you might say to open each topic of conversation with another person.

There's no need to be an expert on the current political scene or the most wanted cars or music, just make sure you have a basic grounding on what people are talking about these days. Here are some other useful thoughts:

- Add to this topic list to include subjects of particular local interest, such as a new traffic system, or subjects that are relevant to the people you talk to often. Copy what other people talk to you about.
- Practise saying your conversation starter out loud a few times, to get the feel for it (and do the same with the open questions from the previous activity). That way you'll be familiar with the sound of your own voice, and it should sound quite natural when you are doing it for real.
- Try your new small talk out on the less important people and situations in your life first – shop assistants, bank tellers, people on the bus or train, or waiters in restaurants.
- Don't worry if you get it wrong to begin with. It will all come naturally with a bit of practice.

## Give your image a boost

Many studies prove what we already know – that others respond to how we dress. A survey of 1,000 people by Friends Reunited Dating showed that the better dressed you are, the more positively other people tend to react. While 42 per cent of respondents preferred a sense of individuality in their prospective partners, some 34 per cent of those surveyed said that they would dump a partner who regularly turned up in wacky clothes, and more than one in ten said they'd refuse a second date if they didn't like what their date wore. Alarmingly, not even ambulance crews are exempt, as another study showed that better-dressed people tended to receive better and swifter care in A&E. This doesn't mean stepping out in a suit every day, of course, but the research indicated that people respond more favourably if you dress smartly and confidently, with an individual style that isn't either too outré or too dowdy. In any case, a bit of a make-over is great for confidence and self-esteem. So go through your wardrobe and get rid of the worthy but uninspiring clothes, the ones you never wear or the impulse buys which never worked out. New shoes or a new outfit can give you a boost.

If you don't want to spend too much, charity shops are a good way to experiment with a new look – you can just give the clothes back a few weeks later if you decide you want something else.

A few more suggestions:

- You could arrange a visit to a personal shopper to get you going (check out if there's a minimum spend, and make sure you can afford it first). Some department stores also have beauty artists keen to try out their make-up on customers.
- If you can afford it, why not treat yourself to a wash and blow dry at the hairdresser instead of doing it yourself? Hairdressers can usually be guaranteed to get you talking. Maybe have your nails done, too. The aim is to treat yourself well and to boost your self-esteem. If money is tight, some of the larger hairstyling academies or beauty colleges often need models for their students and will do your hair for free or for a nominal sum.

## Summary

- Brush up your social skills if you've been out of circulation for a while.
- Be a good listener.
- Think about your image and consider having a mini make-over.
- Be yourself.

# 9

# Finding your perfect partner

In an earlier chapter we discussed the basic human need for a close, intimate and loving bond with another person. There are many reasons why you may not have a 'significant other' or partner to walk beside you. Many people in this position feel there is something missing from their life. Your range of friends and acquaintances may be broad and varied, but you still yearn for someone close to confide in, share sexual intimacy with, and to go through life's ups and downs with. This chapter will give you suggestions on how you might go about finding that special someone. If you lack confidence in yourself, as is an all too natural result of loneliness, do look at the suggestions in the next chapter, which will help you to have more faith in your own abilities to take these ideas forward.

## Relationships

Clare's relationship with James had been going on for about two years. They met at work, and he quickly swept her off her feet. They had even moved into a flat together. He was everything she had ever wanted, and he made her feel special. Then six weeks ago he finished with her. Just like that – a note on the kitchen table when she got home from work. Clare was totally crushed by this, and missed him more than she could put into words. She also felt guilty and rejected, as she was sure it must have been her fault. Clare was now finding her evenings and weekends long and lonely, and her confidence had taken a knock too.

When an important relationship breaks up like this, no words can console us. We are devastated. What we are feeling is emotional loneliness. We have had a satisfying and secure relationship, one which we thought might last. Don't we hope for that with every new relationship? All that most of us want from an intimate relationship is someone we can talk openly with, a feeling of security and tender loving care. The feeling of loss is acute and we feel so alone.

> Dana had been together with Liam for almost 18 months, and they had been looking at houses together. Then, one day, Liam said they needed to talk and asked if they could meet that evening. That wasn't unusual. He often did that. But there was something in his voice. Something was wrong. He came round that evening, and the look on his face and his body language told the same story. It was over. He couldn't really explain it, he said, but it wasn't anything Dana had done, it was definitely him. He had just fallen out of love.

Even if you were the one who finished it, or the relationship just gradually fizzled out and grew stale for both of you, you may still be feeling some of the same loss and disappointment felt by Clare and Dana, whose partners had finished with them completely out of the blue. Because when a relationship breaks up, you lose more than just a loving partner. You lose a way of life, a home, a soul mate, being part of a couple, sexual intimacy, and all the friends and activities you enjoyed as a couple. Then there are all the hopes you may have had for the future.

When forced to choose, many of a couple's friends will just opt out when a relationship breaks up, as they don't want to take sides. This means those friendships may be gone for ever. While you were together, you may have let your own network of friends slip and relied mainly on your partner's friends, so you can be especially lonely if the relationship breaks up. You are no longer one of a pair, with everything that entails. Invitations are so often for couples. Just being with your partner will have contributed to your identity and sense of self too, so you can find yourself feeling completely at sea, all alone and not quite sure who you are any more.

This is a time when there is a special vulnerability to loneliness, both emotional and social. Your confidence in your own ability to go out and meet new potential partners may well be dented. You may feel that getting out and about again in the evenings is something of an effort, but it's an effort worth making in order to avoid becoming lonely. Making new friends and rekindling old friendships is something to do as soon as you can, as it's easier if you make a start quickly, as discussed in Chapter 7. The next chapter will show you how to give yourself renewed confidence in yourself, to make the whole thing less daunting.

## Finding a partner

Though getting back out and about with friends old and new is something to embark on as soon as you feel up to it, don't rush too quickly to find a new partner. Allow time to grieve for the loss and become comfortable in your own skin again. But when you do decide it's time, the worst thing you can do is go out with the thought of finding a partner uppermost in your mind. People will easily work this out and be put off.

No, it's far better to put what you're looking for to the back of your mind and just do the right things. New relationships will then happen on their own, maybe even without you noticing. And the right things to do? Well, simply follow the suggestions in the previous chapter for making friends, and in the next chapter for increasing your self-confidence. This will equip you with a more positive self-image, and something to say for yourself too. Then simply get out there among people. Prince Charming is unlikely to just arrive on your doorstep, though this can happen sometimes. The Duchess of Cambridge's father, Michael Middleton, is reputed to have said in his father-of-the-bride speech at her wedding to Prince William in 2011, 'I knew things were getting serious when I found a Chinook helicopter in my back garden.' But for all of us lesser mortals, Prince Charming is just not a viable option.

Before we think about finding that special person, let's put to rest a common misconception: that is, the idea that opposites attract. Maybe they do, but they don't form satisfying and lasting relationships. In terms of both our potential friends and our potential partners, we tend to get on best with people who are like us – people who think like us, have similar interests, have similar opinions and may even come from a similar background. All these make sustaining a relationship much more likely, indicates research on marital success.

So making friends and meeting people, as we've already talked about in Chapter 7, is your first step. You are then likely to find that you get chatting with someone over a week or two, and if there's a meeting of minds, he or she might suggest doing something together, separate from the others.

## The one and only?

There is a second misconception which needs clarifying. And that is that there is 'the one' out there somewhere, the perfect partner for us, our soul mate, and that we have to find that one person in order to be happy and have a satisfying relationship. This is also not so. There are lots of Mr Rights and Miss Rights out there for each of us. So there are many possibilities. Maybe that's less romantic and less to do with destiny and starry-eyed idealism than many people would like, but it's true. We are most likely to form a strong relationship with someone quite like ourselves, with similar interests and belief systems, and also similar in terms of attractiveness. So there are quite a few out there who will fit that bill. That's how dating agencies work. There may even be 'chemistry' between you and one of these possible partners straight away, but if not it will probably develop gradually as your relationship strengthens and deepens. This may be taking away a little from the thrills and excitement of seeking 'the one', but there is the advantage that it does make it considerably easier for each of us to find our Mr or Miss Right.

If you feel confident enough, you can also take the direct approach and try going to a singles night or speed dating, or go on a singles holiday, but maybe take a friend along too, and use your common sense and intuition to make sure you get the best out of this and don't have any problems. Don't give out any personal details or contact information unless you are very sure.

## Speed dating

Speed dating is usually advertised locally, and is a quick way to get to know around 12 to 15 people enough to decide whether you would want to get to know them more, without any awkwardness or commitment. At speed dating, everyone is given a badge with their name or a number on it, and paper and pen to write notes about each person. Tables for two are set out round the room, and the organizers allow three or four minutes for each pair to talk and ask each other questions, before ringing a bell and asking everyone to move around in such a way as to meet all the potential dates in the room. Afterwards, you indicate in a form, or on the internet back at home, which people you'd be interested in meeting for a date. If they have also ticked your box, then e-mail addresses or phone numbers will be exchanged and you take it from there, still with no commitment to follow through.

## Internet dating

With social networking sites massively popular and the internet being such a powerhouse of communication of all kinds, internet dating sites are not the tacky enterprise you might have imagined. Most people now accept these as an easier way to meet people without going through all the stressful and often time-wasting pre-liminaries. Just as with speed dating, you can tell within minutes, or even moments, of meeting someone if there is any point in pursuing a relationship. Internet dating also cuts out all of that and moves things to next base straight away. You could see it as replacing what used to happen when a girl fell for the boy next door, whom she'd known all her life. The point is that when couples used to meet and form a relationship nearby or in the same small town, they already knew a great deal about each other, as they'd both lived there since they were born, and they knew that this union had possibilities. You could say that internet dating sites just replace all of that pre-date knowledge which modern living has taken away from us. Some tips:

- Check out a few sites before registering with one.
- If you can, use one which has been recommended to you.
- By all means try a free site, but you may find that paying a small fee (currently £10–£30) per month will be value for money.
- You don't need to decide on dating someone straight away: you can exchange a few e-mails with a person and build a relation-ship before trying it out in the real world.
- You don't have to respond to someone's e-mail – the only way you can be contacted is within the site's own messaging system,

so don't give any information which gives away exactly who and where you are.

## Dating safety

- No matter how you originally met your date, you still need to remember your personal safety. The overwhelming majority of speed daters and internet daters, and even someone you've met in a class or dance school, will be ordinary people looking for a loving relationship, just as you are. But there are rotten apples in every barrel, so take care.
- Always meet in a busy public place the first few times.
- Tell someone where you're going and when, and when to expect you back. Let that person know when you do get back.
- Listen to your intuition. If you feel uncomfortable and that something's not right, it probably isn't, so make an excuse and leave.
- Don't give your address and other personal details until you're sure.
- Only go back to yours or theirs when you know the other person really well, but still let someone know what you're doing to begin with.
- All of that said, enjoy!

## First date

It's always a good idea to have a first meeting which involves some kind of activity that takes the focus off you some of the time. You could try bowling, ice-skating, going to a play or a film, cycling, an exhibition, whatever is a shared interest. Or how about a historical or city tour near where you live? Conversation will then be easier and less forced, as there's something to talk about and gaps when you don't need to speak, and you can relax. Having dinner or going for a walk together means having to talk all the time, and is better kept until a later date. You can always have a coffee or a drink after the visit to the museum or fun on the dry ski slope.

Don't be surprised if you feel quite nervous before the date and wish you hadn't agreed to it at all. You might be tempted to text or phone to cancel and say you have the flu. This is all very normal, and it doesn't mean it's the wrong thing to do or that you've made a mistake. It's just a sign that this is important to you and you're anxious for it to go well. It's also partly excitement about something new and different. All absolutely par for the course on a first date. If this does happen, use relaxation or breathing techniques to help you to feel more calm, but don't cancel. You'll find some simple techniques in Chapter 11, and it's all so much worth the effort. You'll feel much better as soon as you start the date. Things also get easier with each date you have.

Remember what's already been suggested about how to use questions, reflect back what's being said, and all of that, and how to talk about yourself. And don't forget, your date may well be nervous and a bit shy too, so don't concentrate entirely on yourself. Think about the other person too. Your questions and what you talk about can be just a bit more personal than with a new friend, and you can say things such as:

- What's your favourite film (or book or music, or whatever)?
- Give me an idea of what your job is like.
- Where did you train for your job?
- Tell me a bit about your family.
- What kind of food do you like?
- Tell me about some of the holidays you've been on.
- Do you have any hobbies?

If it's been a long time and you're not sure of how things are done these days in intimate and sexual relationships, don't be afraid to ask a close and trusted friend or relative. These days, ordinary mainstream magazines and TV programmes are remarkably frank and up-front on the most intimate of subjects, so read a few magazines and watch a bit of daytime TV and you won't need to be unsure of yourself. There's usually a magazine or a TV programme to suit all ages and backgrounds. Best-selling mainstream novels are also a good source for researching. You'll soon get up to speed. But most people coming on to the dating scene for the first time, or after an absence, are likely to be feeling exactly as you are. Age and levels of experience also vary widely. Best not to make any assumptions: take things as they come, always being ready to say if you prefer to slow things down or speed them up. And don't be afraid to admit a bit of naivety in this area of life. It can be very attractive to others. Not everyone is as experienced in this area as you might think. Here are a few other helpful pointers on how dating works these days:

- Both men and women can ask each other out, though many women still don't feel comfortable about doing it.
- For a first meeting, go for something low-key like going out for a coffee, to test the water and see how it goes.
- It's not the rule that the man pays any more, either. Many couples are happy to 'go Dutch' or share the bill, though some-times the person who asked the other out wants to pay. Best thing to do is offer half, but don't insist too much if your date clearly wants to pay. You can always pay for drinks later, or pay the next time. Take each date as it comes and a pattern will emerge to suit the two of you.
- After the date, if a second one hasn't already been set up, go by what feels right when deciding when to get back in touch and how. There are no hard and fast rules about who calls first. If your date did the paying, a thank-you text would not go amiss within 24 hours. If you're not sure, ask yourself what you would expect in your date's position.

Here are some of the do's and don'ts for forming long-lasting friendships and relationships. Read them over and decide which are your strengths already and which you would like to improve on:

*Don't*:
- talk too much, which can be easy if you're nervous – take deep breaths and leave plenty of spaces for the other person to respond;
- form unrealistic expectations of what's possible, especially early in a relationship, or you risk coming across as too needy;
- apologize too much;
- jump to conclusions.

*Do:*
- be a good listener;
- be open minded (not dogmatic);

- keep confidences;
- be welcoming.

## Enjoy

Remember, go out with the simple aim of enjoying yourself, and the rest will all fall into place without you noticing it. Some of the most enduring intimate relationships have grown out of a friendship. And don't be afraid to make a few mistakes along the way. Just put it all down to experience and move on. Better to make a few mistakes as you go along than not to be travelling on the road at all.

## Summary

- Most people would like a satisfactory intimate and loving bond with another person, and can feel emotionally lonely if they don't have this.
- When you feel ready, there are many different ways of meeting someone who may go on to become a new partner.
- Be aware of the main do's and don'ts for a good relationship.
- Bring yourself up to speed about dating and first dates, especially what to expect and how to keep yourself safe.

# 10

## Building confidence

If you feel lonely, your self-esteem and self-confidence can begin to suffer, even without you noticing it. As we've seen, it's very common for people to blame themselves for being lonely, and consequently to feel rejected and unworthy. Poor self-confidence can itself bring about loneliness, as it makes it more difficult to make friends or keep relationships going. So it's not surprising if, after a period of prolonged loneliness, you begin to lose faith in yourself. But this process works in the other direction too. Both loneliness and low self-esteem are reversible. So tackling low self-confidence is a must.

Bear in mind that appearances can be deceptive. The person we perceive to be most self-assured may actually be the one who lacks confidence. Sometimes the noisy extrovert at the office has a crippling lack of confidence and is using this display of bravado as a smokescreen. Many comedians and impressionists learned their skills to mask shyness and uncertainty at school, or to avoid being bullied.

Despite a good display of outward confidence, many people have doubts and insecurities about themselves. They have just become good at camouflaging these over the years. Or they've become good at only doing the things they feel they cope well with, and staying in their comfort zone. Few people are confident about every aspect of their lives.

Always remember that loneliness is not your fault, and that many people feel exactly as you do right now – some of them even live in your street. So there's absolutely no need to feel rejected or left out. Maybe your particular situation has meant you're lonely, and you've felt you had little or no control over this. What this book is about is taking control back and making simple changes to relieve that loneliness. It's about having a different mindset, and a different approach.

## A new approach

Building confidence underlies much of that change of mindset, and it may require you to make some changes. But these don't need to be big changes, or difficult changes. A small change here and there can make huge differences. And these changes might just be in the way you think about yourself, how you think about the people you know, or your understanding of what being confident is all about.

Becoming more confident is not something that will happen overnight. Losing your confidence probably took some time to happen, so it will take a bit of time to re-build it too. But each step will see confidence beginning to return. Reading this book is the first of those steps, and will show you how to take the next, and the next.

## What is confidence?

But what is confidence? Why is it sometimes so elusive? When you have it you don't notice it at all, but when you lose it you most certainly notice its absence. Why does it seem to come so easily to other people? When you have to walk into a room of strangers, you wonder why it's so difficult for you, and yet everyone else appears to think nothing of it at all. Maybe it's trying to make friends or find a partner. Maybe you can't seem to get a conversation going when you bump into someone you know in the street, or over lunch with work colleagues. Whatever it is, you wonder why you are so self-conscious while everyone else appears to be so relaxed and self-assured. It may help to consider the following points.

### Confidence is goal-related

Self-confidence can be broadly described as our expectations of success in a given field – for example, how well we hope to do in a love affair or an exam. Canadian-born psychologist Dr Albert Bandura has called this belief in our competence – the belief in one's ability to succeed in specific situations – 'self-efficacy expectations'. According to this theory, people with high self-efficacy are more likely to view obstacles as stepping stones.

## Confidence is situational

Self-confidence varies from task to task – for example, Phillip is at home with computers but a waste of space when it comes to gardening; Jean handles cats with ease but distrusts dogs and people; Angela is a confident nurse in A&E but very shy, both about meeting new people and in keeping up with old friends.

## What does being confident mean to you?

With these points in mind, give the following exercise a try:

1 What is confidence? It can sometimes be hard to put this into words or images. Have a try at this now. Think of exactly what you are aiming for. What does being confident mean to you? Which main things do you want to be able to do, or do better? Take as long as you need to think about this, then write it down in your notebook. For example, Paul's list looked like this:
   - Good at tennis if a bit too aggressive in my game.
   - Bad at the socializing that goes with it.
   - Goal: to enjoy chatting to people after a tennis game, i.e. to buy my tennis partner a drink or join in one of the club's afternoon teas.

   Angela's list ran as follows:
   - Cool and competent in an emergency, I know just what to say to patients and am not fazed by trauma.
   - No idea how to relate to colleagues off-duty; spend free time alone and all too often drinking a beer in front of the TV, on the excuse that my shifts make socializing impossible.
   - Goal: to tidy the house, which is a slob's palace, so I can invite people round, and to join a ramblers' club both to socialize and to lose some weight.

2 Now try imagining, as clearly as you can, what it would feel like to be more confident. Try to visualize the feelings as vividly as you can. What would having confidence mean you could do that you can't do now? What differences would it make in your relationships, or your work, or socially? Take time to think about these questions for a few moments, and again write the answers down.

Some people are better at imagining things than others. But even if you didn't get a clear image, this exercise should help you get a flavour of what you want to achieve. Don't worry if it was all just a blur, and impossible to get a fix on any of these ideas. Just trying to get in touch with your goal is helpful, and there's plenty of time to make that picture come into sharper focus.

### How a confident person behaves

Here are a few ideas of how a confident person behaves socially:

- Can be lively and outgoing, but can also be quiet and thoughtful, depending on the situation.
- Is open, welcoming and genuine to talk to.
- Listens actively to other people when they are talking.
- Enjoys listening to and talking to other people.
- Enjoys socializing with other people.

But remember that very few, if any, people match this description of a confident person. Even the most confident people we know will fall short on one or more of these characteristics. They just hide their weaknesses well.

## Can you be too confident?

But what about being too confident? No doubt you've heard criticisms of others who are 'getting too big for their boots', and this might make you concerned about becoming over-confident.

Of course, it is the fear that their children will become 'too big for their boots' or conceited and arrogant that has partly driven the parental style of praising little and criticizing often. But giving praise when it's due does not have this effect at all. In fact it's the complete opposite. Praise given appropriately helps to maintain a healthy self-esteem, not produce over-confidence. Unconditional love and affection do the same. No, withholding praise but giving criticism has the very damaging effect of substantially reducing confidence in children, who then grow up as adults with a poor self-image.

This can happen to us as adults too if a close friend or a partner behaves in a similar way, constantly criticizing and blaming, with only occasional praise and compliments, and with love and affection conditional on 'good' behaviour. Spending long hours alone can have the same effect, as you feel guilty, blame yourself and beat yourself up about all the things you feel you must be doing wrong to be alone like this.

## How do you see yourself?

How you see yourself is usually at the heart of the problem, and people who lack confidence often have a poor self-image. This is tied closely to feelings of low self-esteem. This negative self-image is a perception of yourself you have developed as a result of your experiences in life, and usually bears little relation to the real person. It's as if you are perpetually looking at yourself through one of those distorting mirrors they used to have at the fun fair. What you need to do is to stop looking at a distorted image and see yourself in a true mirror. Sometimes, rather than having a negative self-image, people with low confidence can simply have an unclear picture of who and what they really are. It's as if they are looking in a mirror in a poorly lit room, and are finding it hard to see themselves at all.

## List your achievements

Bearing in mind that confidence tends to be related to specific situations, we need to be aware that sometimes when we lack confidence we have lost sight of the fact that we have achieved things in our lives. While everyone has achievements, the difference in those who lack confidence is that they tend to forget theirs, or think that they don't count for some reason, or brush them off as 'just luck'. We may feel that it's arrogant or swollen-headed to be pleased with something we've done.

These are all thoughts which tend to appear when someone is lonely or lacking confidence. The truth is, your achievements are your achievements and are down to you. They are for you to be proud and satisfied about. But this goes further than thinking that your achievements don't count. It's also about not recognizing and acknowledging them – often it's easy to overlook your own achievements, perhaps feeling they're too mundane or common to be of note. Or, if you're overly modest, or have been alone too long, you might tend to play down your skills and accomplishments, feeling they have little relevance – people without enough social back-up don't tend to realize how successful they've been because there's no-one to tell them. We all need others to reflect and acknowledge what we've done.

I hope the following activity will help you to see your achievements in a more positive light. So, go through the achievements listed, and make a list of those which apply to you. Add some more as you think of them.

## My achievements

*Life achievements*, for example:

- Brought up a child – alone or with help.
- Cared for an older relative or friend.
- Stuck with a demanding job or completed an important work project.
- Travelled abroad.
- Acquired everyday skills, e.g. using a computer, learning to drive.
- Other things you can feel proud of, e.g. arranging a wedding or funeral, settling a child into university.

*Areas of expertise*, for example:

- Completed a course or training of some kind.
- Gained knowledge of a specialist hobby or pastime, e.g. birds, sport, languages, embroidery.
- Written a story, poem, article or book.
- Learned to play a musical instrument.
- Acquired practical home skills – cooking, decorating, gardening, etc.

*Social accomplishments*, for example:

- Been a good friend to someone.
- Been an active member of a club or organization.
- Become involved in a community project or a charity.
- Raised money for a good cause.

*Special achievements*: these are the fleeting moments we often take for granted, minor unexpected events, or achievements that only have meaning for us and can't be measured by the outside world. Watching the sunset, random acts of kindness and time spent with a special friend might be examples. Here are ideas from some of the people interviewed for this book:

- Wrapping up a child's birthday present beautifully.
- Taking an extra five minutes to complete a work task.
- Giving money to a drummer playing for charity, and staying to listen!
- Learning a little about a friend's area of interest so as to relate to her better.
- Choosing an outfit that works.
- Watching sparrows have a dustbath on a hot summer's day.

Now list your own examples in your notebook. It's easy once you get going.

## Your skills, strengths and talents

A false conclusion of those with poor self-esteem is that they have few skills, or that everyone else does it better. As you can see from the preceding exercise, the truth is that we all have skills which we use every day but which we take for granted.

Table 10.1 is another exercise to help you become more aware of skills, talents and strengths. Take your time and work your way through it; it may help to have your notebook handy and jot down any item you feel applies to you. Don't soul-search too much on the answers, just mull over how you are in general, most days, on each item. Remember, no modesty allowed!

## Body language

Look around on a bus or train, or at the shops or work, and you'll realize how we all make judgements about each other based purely on body language. A mass of silent information about other people is constantly being processed by us and we come to conclusions, the majority of which will be spot on. A colleague who is nervous

## Table 10.1  Skills, talents and strengths

| | |
|---|---|
| *Personal* | • Determined<br>• Honest<br>• Patient<br>• Having a sense of humour<br>• Caring<br>• Considerate<br>• Having natural warmth<br>• Confident<br>• Sensible<br>• Positive<br>• Trustworthy<br>• Hard-working |
| *Social* | • Friendly<br>• Sensitive to other people's moods<br>• Tactful<br>• Able to get on with other people<br>• Able to express feelings<br>• Good at listening to others<br>• Reliable |
| *Thinking and learning* | • Good at learning new things<br>• A quick and clear thinker<br>• Having ideas<br>• Imaginative<br>• Good at analysing things<br>• Able to solve problems |
| *Physical* | • Keeping fit<br>• Keeping strong<br>• Staying calm under pressure<br>• Looking good<br>• Having lots of energy<br>• Being good at a sport or other activity |
| *Practical* | • Being good at mending things<br>• Being able to work steadily<br>• Being able to work with computers<br>• Being able to cook<br>• Skilled at DIY |
| *Artistic/creative* | • Having creative writing skills<br>• Musical<br>• A dancer<br>• Having painting skills<br>• Being good at drama<br>• A gardener |

| *Practical communication* | ● Able to explain things clearly in writing |
| | ● Good at writing letters |
| | ● Can text |
| | ● Can e-mail |
| | ● Able to explain things clearly by voice |
| *Practical organization* | ● Efficient |
| | ● Paying attention to detail |
| | ● Being logical |
| | ● Good with figures |
| | ● Able to organize time |
| | ● Able to co-ordinate lots of things |
| | ● Able to complete tasks on time |
| *Leadership* | ● Taking the lead when needed |
| | ● Staying calm in a crisis |
| | ● Taking the initiative |
| | ● Able to organize people |

because he has an important appraisal meeting today; a teenager in school uniform on the bus who clearly would prefer to be going anywhere but school. This isn't voyeurism – it's an important part of being human. As a species we learned body language long before there was the spoken word. We had to, in order to survive and live as a highly social species.

To some extent this is an automatic process. We tend to interpret body language without thinking, and are usually unaware of how other people's body language is affecting us. We are just aware of the conclusions we are drawing from it. We have all seen and heard people engaged in conversation at a bit of a distance, across the street or at the other side of a room, and even without hearing the actual words they are using we can make a pretty good stab at working out what is going on – an argument, a discussion, romance, everyday conversation, and so on. If a group of young people approach us on the street, it's body language that tells us instantly whether this is nothing to concern ourselves about or whether we feel intimidated.

So lack of confidence will show through body language. It then becomes a vicious circle, because others will read this instantly and react accordingly. How do people react to you if you come over as shy and perhaps nervous, maybe avoiding eye contact and sitting in a corner? Many people will ignore you, not because they don't like you or consider that you're a bad person, but because they feel awkward and they don't know what to say to you. Most people will take the easier route and talk to someone else instead. This will make you feel even more rejected and even less confident, which will show in your body language, and so it goes on.

But it's easy to do something about that. If you can improve your feeling of self-worth and increase your understanding of who you are, this will automatically show in your body language. This is how good actors can become such different people so easily, working to get the posture, voice and body language just right. Be like a good actor by changing your body language to that of a confident person. Here are some ideas on how to appear calm and quietly confident:

- Take a bit of time out to think about your own body language. Find a full-length mirror for this, or use a video camera – this can be a bit of a shock, but effective.
- Stand in front of a full-length mirror as you would normally stand, without thinking about it too much. I know this all sounds odd, and you'll feel self-conscious, but it does help. Look at yourself closely. Take a few moments. How were you standing? Try to take a step outside of yourself for a moment to think. Be a fly on the wall. Imagine you are in a TV programme. What impression are you giving? Be honest.
- Now move to the side and walk past the mirror in your usual walking style, looking at your reflection as you pass. Turn and walk back again in the other direction. How did you walk past the mirror? What image is this giving?
- How do you come into a room? Position your full-length mirror to check this out if you can. Go out of the room now, close the door, then come back into the room, the way you would if you were going into a meeting where five or six people were already comfortably seated and you didn't know any of them. Take a moment or two before you do this, to try to imagine the scenario really clearly and vividly, and feel the way you would be feeling. Now think about how you came through the door:
  - What was your body posture (upright, stooped, head up)?
  - What speed were you moving (tentative, fast, slow)?

- Did you come halfway in then hold back a little? Or what?
- How far did you open the door?
- Where were your arms and what were they doing (e.g. by your sides, in pockets, holding on to something for comfort)?
- What about eye contact when you came into the room? Where were you looking?

Now think about confident people you know – how would they come into the same room, in the same situation? Think about it using these same headings.

You can practise this at home when no-one's about, until you get a feel for it. With a bit of practice it will become you, and you won't need to think about it. The best of it is that if you stand and walk confidently, you will actually feel and be more confident. So it's a win–win situation. Try it and see.

## Don't try to do too much all at once

Don't jump in at the deep end. If you try to remember all these ideas about body language all at once, you'll come into a room looking preoccupied, and maybe slightly confused! Not a good idea. It's best to concentrate on one thing at a time, maybe your general posture, and work on that for a while before moving on, maybe to what you're doing with your hands, your head or your eyes. Body language is the habit of a lifetime. It takes a little time and effort to make changes. But the positive side of this is that, with each change, the next one comes a little more easily, and the feedback of improvements in how other people react to these changes is also likely to encourage you and improve your confidence in what you're doing. So the only way is up.

## Insecurity

Non-confident body language comes about mainly from a feeling of insecurity and the need for some kind of 'comforter'. We are nervous, ill at ease and unsure of ourselves and, just like children, might seek comfort from contact with another person or object, for example clinging to a handbag or a cigarette or a pen, or making sure we have someone beside us at social events. A wish to make ourselves as small and unnoticeable as possible makes us hunch up our shoulders, stoop slightly and avoid eye contact.

## So what can we do to make things better?

An open and relaxed posture is best. Open posture means standing or sitting comfortably upright, with shoulders comfortably back and head up. Slouching into a chair or a corner can be comforting but looks defensive and uninviting. Sit up and lean forward a little towards others when talking. This shows interest and encourages people to talk to you. Don't fold your arms or place them across yourself, as this may be perceived as a barrier or a lack of interest, or even disagreement. Crossed legs or ankles also tend to appear defensive or negative. Nervous tension can make you form a fist with your hands or cling tightly to a handbag, briefcase or drink. This may be noticed unconsciously, or even consciously, by those you are with. Better to have arms comfortably by your side, or open hands resting easily on your lap when sitting. This conveys quiet and relaxed self-assurance. The relaxation and breathing exercises you will meet in Chapter 11 will make this posture easier to achieve, so remember to practise these.

## Appearance

Have another good look at yourself in the mirror. But this time concentrate on your appearance in terms of clothing, weight, make-up and jewellery (if you wear any). We are often just in too big a hurry to notice ourselves in this way.

So have a good look, in the mirror or at recent photos or videos of yourself. Look at them coldly and objectively. Look around at other people of a similar age and background. How are they looking? What are they wearing? Any changes you would like to make? Weight, style, fitness, hair, clothes, whatever. A new healthy, fit and more modern look, and if necessary losing or gaining a few pounds too, can make a huge difference to your confidence.

## Eye contact

When you're unsure of yourself, it can be easier to look at the floor or out of the window when talking to someone, only making eye contact occasionally, if at all. At the other extreme, some people might overdo it, with a fixed stare. Either way, the other person feels uncomfortable.

For everyday socializing, making eye contact for about two-thirds of the time is usually appropriate, but judge what feels right for you. Women tend to use eye contact a little more than men do. On a first meeting with someone, a general guideline would be to look for three to four seconds, then glance away for one to two seconds, then look back for another three to four seconds, and so on. It's probably better to look more when you're listening, and look away more when you're talking. It's also better to break eye contact in a downward direction, as this shows interest. Breaking eye contact in an upward or sideways direction or keeping eye contact for too long can seem disconcerting or negative. You could try these different eye contact styles on a friend and ask how he or she feels.

Again, don't try to make too many changes to your body language all at once, but, as before, a bit of practice with this will improve things if it is a problem for you. Best to practise in situations which are less important first.

## Tone of voice

Almost as important as your body language is your voice and how you use it. Body language and tone of voice together convey most of what we communicate to others. Being on your own a lot will mean you have long periods of not using your voice at all, so when you do speak it can sound somewhat unfamiliar.

Tone of voice is important – aim for a gentle, low-pitched and friendly tone. It is often a person's warm and welcoming tone of voice that makes others perceive them as friendly or a 'good listener'. If you're not sure how you sound, try making a recording and have a listen.

Here is a way of making your tone of voice become more interesting and more confident. You can practise this whenever you want if you find it helpful. If you have an audio recorder or video recorder, you could record this to see how you do, but you don't need to do this. Listening to the sound of your own voice is a great confidence-builder.

This exercise is worth practising often if you feel your voice needs work on it, or if your confidence when speaking needs building. It also helps to get you used to the sound of your own voice and, more than that, used to hearing your own confident voice. It's a great starting point. Here's what to do:

- If you have young children around, choose one of their books, sit one or more of them down and read a story aloud to them. If not, just find a book of children's stories and read it out loud on your own. Read it to your pet if you have one.
- As you read, try to add as much interest to it as you can, using your voice alone. Remember how actors read stories to children on TV, and let your voice reflect what's happening in the story. The emotions, the danger, the action. Change the pace, the volume, the pitch, the tone. Do voices for each character. Don't be self-conscious – anything will do. Children will love it no matter what you do. Remember how you used to talk to your friends in the school playground? You can do it. No holds barred! If it's difficult at first, you'll improve with practice.
- If there's no pet or child around, you can try reading the first few lines of each news item in the newspaper as if you were the newsreader, doing it for real.
- You can also put the subtitles on if you're watching TV, then turn the sound off and read what those in the programme are saying to each other, adding in the feelings and adapting your tone of voice to suit. Better still, just turn off the sound and make up what the people might be saying – this can be quite funny.

## Cultural differences

It is worth bearing in mind that all that has been said so far about body language is most likely to apply for two people from the same cultural background and in a Western-type society. When people from the same cultural or ethnic background interact with one another, they can very easily read each other's body language, as they share that language. But each cultural background has its own specific body language, especially with respect to gestures, personal space and comforting. Even a nod of the head can have a different meaning.

## Getting the body talk right

Table 10.2 is a checklist of ways of appearing confident through body language. Remember, if you follow the descriptions here, you will appear more self-assured and at ease with yourself, even if you don't feel it inside.

## Take it slowly

Don't go overboard. Concentrate on changing one thing at a time. You can always refer back to this book for more ideas, once you've mastered a few changes.

## Summary

- For some people, being alone a great deal lowers their self-confidence.
- A lack of confidence isn't always as obvious to others as you think. Many people lack confidence, even if they appear extrovert, but hide this well. Everyone lacks confidence in something.
- Remember you have achievements, strengths, skills and talents to be proud of.
- You can easily use body language to appear and feel more confident.

**Table 10.2 Confident body language**

| | |
|---|---|
| *Body* | • Comfortably upright posture<br>• Head comfortably up<br>• Shoulders relaxed, down and back<br>• Regular and direct eye contact (about two-thirds of the time)<br>• Relaxed<br>• Little or nothing in hands<br>• No barriers with hands or arms<br>• Give people their space<br>• Respect cultural differences |
| *Impressions* | • First impressions do matter, so give a good one<br>• Walk the walk<br>• Talk the talk |
| *Clothing and appearance* | • Loose and comfortable<br>• Layers best for all temperature conditions<br>• Suited to the situation<br>• Smart and clean<br>• Hair neat and presentable<br>• Style up to date but not over the top |
| *Entering a room* | • Think before you go in, and get your posture and appearance right<br>• Open the door firmly<br>• Enter with confidence<br>• Enter as if you mean it<br>• Make eye contact immediately with those in the room |
| *Voice* | • Slow<br>• Steady<br>• Low-pitched<br>• Warm |
| *Handshakes* | • Relaxed but firm<br>• Not limp |
| *Habits to avoid* | • Hands in pockets<br>• Fiddling with anything (pen, jewellery, money, clothing)<br>• Clutching for comfort (handbag, pen, notes, etc.)<br>• Slouching<br>• Too many gestures |

# 11

# More ways to overcome loneliness

I hope you now have a better understanding about different kinds of loneliness, the way loneliness comes about and how natural it is. I also hope you've found it helpful to look at the suggestions on how to make more friends, find a partner and improve your self-confidence.

In this chapter there are a few loose ends to tie up. How do you look after yourself when there's no-one else around to do it, and how can you cope better with stress? What about special times such as Christmas, bank holiday weekends and Valentine's Day? And what do you do if you've tried everything and it's just not working, or you're feeling so lonely and low that any effort is just too much?

## Positive mental attitude

You may have heard of a 'positive mental attitude', an old idea put into words and made popular by two Americans: motivational author Napoleon Hill and successful businessman W. Clement Stone. But whatever name you give to it, being positive and optimistic will make you feel better and will encourage people to want to know more about you. Unfortunately, as you would expect, loneliness tends to produce the opposite kinds of feelings. But you can change that, little by little.

- Try to be positive and up-beat when you talk with people. If you don't feel it at first, just pretend – 'fake it to make it' or 'act as if'. People can't tell the difference. Acting positively does actually make you feel more positive, too. Negative people are off-putting. None of us enjoy talking to someone who is pessimistic and downbeat. So making the effort to be optimistic and smile will bring you good results. Positivity will take hold and grow with you, and it will become easier each day.

- Balance your time so sometimes you are with people and sometimes you are alone. We all need the right mixture of solitude and company. Plan ahead what to do when you're alone. Work towards being happy in your own skin.
- Work out whether you prefer to talk in a group or to have one-to-one conversations, or a mixture of the two. Start with situations that are easiest for you. There's no need to make things more difficult than they need to be.
- Remember, it's not just you who feels lonely. So look around – many of those you see will also be lonely and will be putting on a face to hide behind. They'll welcome your smile or conversation, just as you will welcome theirs.

## Look after yourself

Taking good care of yourself physically and emotionally is going to encourage others to care for you. After all, how do you react to someone you meet who appears downbeat and lacking in self-respect? Compare that with a positive person who clearly looks after him or herself.

Start by working towards a healthier diet if you need to, and avoiding too much coffee or alcohol. It's so easy to comfort eat or have that extra drink when you're bored and lonely and there's no-one around to see you having that chocolate bar or filling up your glass again. The same goes for fitness levels. If you're feeling low and that no-one cares, getting up from the sofa and going for a walk or going to the gym is incredibly difficult. But it all helps to lift your spirits, put a smile on your face and make you look as if you value yourself, and these are all very attractive features which draw others to you. Look in the mirror and put on a smile, and see what a difference that makes to how you appear. It doesn't matter if you don't mean the smile or feel the positivity yet, as long as you look as if you do – that will draw people to you. Eating healthily and improving your fitness level will also help you to feel generally more relaxed, which is also a very attractive feature.

## Coping with stress

Being lonely is very stressful. Sometimes, too, thinking about breaking out from loneliness can add to that stress, even as you build up the motivation and the energy to do so. Some straight-forward ways to manage stress can help to build resilience before making a first step, until confidence grows.

Here are two simple relaxation techniques, 'Breathing counts', and 'Body check'. These are both good to use for a couple of minutes every hour or so throughout the day to reduce feelings of stress or anxiety. No-one needs to know what you're doing. They're quite invisible to other people. Only you will know what you're doing. You can also use them any time, anywhere, to help stay calm and relaxed exactly when you want to be:

**Breathing counts**

1 Lie down, or sit in a chair with good support, or stand still with your arms relaxed by your side.
2 Let your breath go, then take a gentle breath in, and place on that inward breath your own slow and silent count of 1 . . . 2 . . . 3 . . .
3 Then, in your own time, breathe out, placing on this outward breath the same slow and silent count of 1 . . . 2 . . . 3 . . .
4 Continue gently breathing to this rhythm for a minute or two.

**Body check**

1 Lie down, or sit in a chair with good support, or stand still with your arms relaxed by your side.
2 Take a deep breath in, and while breathing in silently check all over your body for any signs of tension. Start from the top of your head and check all the way down to the tips of your toes.
3 As you breathe out again, just relax and release any tension you have found in your body.
4 Repeat 2 and 3 once more.

## Holidays

Loneliness is notoriously difficult at holiday periods, such as Christmas and bank holiday weekends, and on special days like your birthday or Valentine's Day. Remember, it's not just you, and despite the way the television, newspapers and magazines present it, everyone isn't having a super time with family and friends. Many are lonely, and many are working too.

Holidays are not what they used to be. In December 2010, *The Lancet* published its Wakley Prize-winning essay, 'An epidemic of loneliness', written by Dr Ishani Kar-Purkayastha from the UK Health Protection Agency. Dr Kar-Purkayastha had based the essay on a patient she referred to as Doris, who was complaining of a number of non-existent symptoms so that she could stay in hospital over Christmas, rather than return to an empty house. Doris had been a widow for 20 years, and her children lived abroad.

On the other hand, I know several people who regularly spend Christmas alone, but who make the most of it and rather enjoy having a day on the sofa, eating what and when they want, choosing all their favourite meals, and being able to watch whatever they like on television – and in fact having time to watch it, instead of slaving over a hot stove making Christmas lunch.

If you dread bank holidays, birthdays or other 'special' days, here are some suggestions:

- If friends or family members ask you to join them, say yes. It doesn't matter if you think they're only doing it because they feel sorry for you or they don't really mean it. What does that matter? An invitation is an invitation. So say yes, be positive and enjoy yourself, help out with the cooking and the washing up, relax and be part of the event.
- If you can afford it, treat yourself to a singles holiday at those special times of year, or arrange to stay in a hotel where there will be company.
- Be on the look-out for others in your position and ask them over to yours, or go out together for a drink or a meal.
- Check out if the local church or a charity is putting on anything for people in your position.
- Treat yourself to some really nice presents. Or parcel some up

beautifully and donate them to a local charity or hospital, and make a difference.

- Do some volunteering at a soup kitchen or shelter for the homeless. Helping others who are worse off than yourself helps to keep these things in proportion.

## If it all gets too much

Sometimes, despite trying everything, the loneliness just won't shift. Maybe you feel powerless to do anything about it any more. Maybe you are desperately lonely and have been for some time, and you feel an aching sense of isolation. In such circumstances, have a check-up with the doctor and explain how you've been feeling. There can be physical reasons for feeling this way, and it's possible you are experiencing depression. The doctor will be able to treat such problems and help you to recover. There are 'talking therapies' which can help people to cope better with long-term desperate loneliness, and with depression.

## Keeping going and coping with setbacks

Hard as it can be to initiate change, the benefits of making changes to your life soon make themselves felt. Nothing motivates you to keep going like success. Of course, it can't all be plain sailing. Nothing works that way. In fact, you're highly likely to meet setbacks. It's well known that setbacks are more likely to occur in the first few months after making a change.

So be prepared for hiccups and setbacks. Even the most highly motivated and enthusiastic person, who is doing all the right things, has days when nothing goes right. But be assured, we all have days like that, no matter who we are and what we do in life. It may be a question of two steps forward, one step back. But this is to be expected, so don't be put off by it. You regain any ground lost much more quickly after a setback, so there's no question of being back to the start again. Just keep going, and you will get there.

- If you've had a setback, give yourself a breather. Rest, relax, recruit your strength. Don't rush back into the battlefield. Take a few days to get things into perspective, and then decide what you want to do.

- Write down what you learn from any setback. Use what you write down to see if there's any pattern to setbacks. For example, are you keeping expectations realistic? Are you maybe hoping to change too much too soon? Don't forget to celebrate the small successes – they're actually big steps towards where you want to be.

- Make a big, bold wish-list. Writing down what you want is an important part of the process of receiving it. Out of sight is often out of mind where plans are concerned, so have it in large brightly coloured print on a poster-size sheet of paper and display this prominently. For more private or confidential plans, write them on a card and keep them somewhere only you will see them. Be as creative as you like with this one, and use any artistic or computer skills to personalize your plan.

- Don't forget small steps. You're much more likely to be successful if you just have one new thing to do at a time. So make that wish-list, but take your wishes one at a time.

- Write down a list of the benefits you will gain from your plans – things like self-respect, achievement, less loneliness and, of course, more friends. Read the list regularly, and especially if you're tempted to give up.

- If you're lucky enough to know someone suitable, ask a trustworthy friend to act as your 'mentor' or 'supporter' to encourage you when you are tempted to let things slip.

### Give it time

Not only does it take time to build friendships, there's also research to show that it takes time to get over loneliness itself. Research by John Cacioppo shows that symptoms of depression associated with loneliness can long outlast the condition itself – by as much as two years. On the positive side, the reverse is also true – the good effects of feeling connected also persist for two years, even if those relationships falter.

## Tackle unhelpful thinking

Be ready for the voice at the back of your mind saying things which might put you off making the changes you need to make to overcome loneliness. These thoughts coming from the back of your mind are the voice of your anxiety about change. You can change that voice, and make it more positive and encouraging.

How you think has a very powerful effect on the choices and decisions you make every day, probably more powerful than you know. A meta-analysis of nearly 40 years of loneliness research suggested that the best way to reduce people's loneliness is via training in 'social cognition' – changing negative thoughts about themselves and how others perceive them. Dr Christopher Masi and co-authors at the University of Chicago Medical Center analysed every study on loneliness from between 1970 and 2009 and considered four types of solutions:

- 'Social contact' – bringing lonely people together in person or via e-mail
- 'Social support' – from visitors, group activities or pets
- Teaching social skills
- 'Social cognition' – the ability to understand and navigate social interactions. This last was the most promising.

So, when you find yourself thinking 'unhelpful thoughts' such as, 'I can't do this' or 'Nobody will talk to me' or 'It's not worth the effort', question and challenge these thoughts by asking yourself the following questions, and answering them honestly:

1 What is the evidence for this thought?
2 Is there any evidence against this thought?
3 Who says it's true anyway?
4 What would I tell a friend if he or she were in the same situation and thinking this thought?

So, for example, if you are thinking 'No-one will talk to me' before going to a course on computer skills, your answers to these four questions might be:

1 None.
2 Lots.

3 Just me.

4 I'd tell him that most people feel a bit nervous going to something new, but that soon passes, and that of course people will talk to him. People always talk to each other on courses. The tutor will usually encourage working in small groups too. I'd tell him he should go and enjoy himself. I might also say that he is a really nice and interesting person, and people will like him for sure. And I'd say it's really worth the effort.

## Developing self-reliance

Are other people always the answer? Do we always have to rely on others for fun and enjoyment? We've already discussed how solitude can be fertile in terms of creativity and contentment. It's also important to develop faith in yourself and your own abilities. Get to know yourself better, and what your interests and priorities are. We began this earlier in the book, and you can take this forward. Be on the look-out for new interests and pastimes which create enjoyment and satisfaction just for you. This in turn will make you more attractive to potential friends or partners. Being too needy and too dependent definitely discourages friendships. Trust your own judgement. You know what you want better than anyone else. Work towards becoming your own best friend, who will always be there for you no matter what happens.

## Summary

- There are many ways you can cope better with holiday periods and 'special days'.
- Be good to yourself and stay well physically and mentally. Learn to relax and cope better with the stresses of life.
- Be prepared for setbacks.
- Tackle unhelpful thinking.

# Conclusion

As we've seen, beating loneliness starts and continues with just one small step. It's up to you. You can try your first step and then wait until you feel comfortable with how that is going. Then you can decide on the next step, and so on. So there will only ever be one first step, and that first step will be something small and manageable, and something you've thought about and chosen for yourself. And then it's similar bite-size steps thereafter, always under your control. There's no need to hurry. Take the time you need. Too many changes too quickly can be stressful, and you're probably already feeling tense and anxious because of the loneliness, so there's no point in adding to that.

## 'Future-proof' yourself against loneliness

The Campaign to End Loneliness produced a booklet called 'Safeguarding the Convoy' (2010). Professor Jenny de Jong Gierveld, professor emeritus in sociology and social gerontology at VU University Amsterdam, introduced the concept of the 'convoy', our personal 'convoy' of friends, family, work relationships, acquaintances, interests and pastimes and possessions, which accompanies us through life, creating and maintaining our identity and self-confidence. Professor Gierveld stresses that in order to combat loneliness in the long term, everyone in society, including individuals, the voluntary sector, authorities and services, both national and local, should work to 'safeguard the convoy' for us all.

So how do you 'future-proof' yourself against loneliness? This depends to a large extent on where you live and the type of loneliness you want to guard against, but, while there are no guarantees, you can reduce the risk of loneliness in the future immensely, both for yourself and for others. Given that there are millions of lonely people across all age groups, it's important that we all work together on this for a better future for everyone:

- Continually renew and refresh your current relationships – keep your social circle as wide as you can. This takes time and energy, but it is definitely worth it. Plan for the future. It may not seem to matter today, but it will matter in years to come.

- Keep up with the times in terms of communication. Currently that would mean making sure you can text and e-mail, and acquaint yourself with social networking sites if you haven't already. Of course, the future will turn up more new ways of communicating, so try to keep up with those, even if it seems difficult and not worth the effort.

- Keep an eye on what's happening locally in terms of local services and resources. You may not need these now, but you probably will as years go on. So this is relevant to you. Yes, you may move several times in the years ahead, but if we all look after the area we live in at the time, we're safeguarding resources across the whole country, for everyone, so that wherever you are when you need them, the resources and facilities are there for you. Do whatever you can to help to maintain the opportunities for real social interaction in your area for all ages; and try to create new ones too – this might mean through community action, volunteering for a local charity, campaigning or working with local or national government. Support befriending schemes, bereavement support projects, lunch clubs, community cafes, day centres.

- Work to ensure that there are fewer barriers to people getting out and about and meeting together in your area – for example, fear of crime, poor public transport systems, mobility difficulties for the physically disabled.

- Work towards age barriers being broken down too, so that all ages can mix socially. Older people with time on their hands could help out younger ones who need support such as odd jobs, gardening, occasional childcare. Encourage making use of older people's skills and knowledge, through local history groups, reminiscence groups, fitness clubs, the University of the Third Age. Skilled older people could pass these on to younger people, e.g. painting and decorating, gardening, local crafts, car maintenance, woodwork, and so on. Young people can encourage their elders to keep up with the new technologies and make their 'first click', and whatever the future holds for us in an increasingly electronic world.

Finally, the important thing to say here is that if you're lonely, I don't want you to just *think* about making changes and taking action. You owe it to yourself to go further than just thinking about it, and actually make a start to making your life a less lonely one. Because you are most definitely worth it! And always remember, even if you are on your own or feel as if you're on your own, you are never truly alone, as not far from you there are always people like me, ready and willing to listen, to give you a helping hand along the way, and to care.

Whatever your reason for reading this book, I hope you've found something of what you were looking for. If you've been reading for interest, or as part of a training course, I hope you've learned much that you'll find useful in the future.

# Useful addresses

## Organizations

**ADFAM**
25 Corsham Street
London N1 6DR
Tel.: 020 7553 7640
Website: www.adfam.org.uk
National charity for families and friends of drug users.

**Age UK**
Tavis House
1–6 Tavistock Square
London WC1H 9NA
Tel.: 0800 169 8787 (helpline)
Website: www.ageuk.org.uk

**Alcoholics Anonymous**
The Flower House
3–5 Cynthia Street
London N1 9JF
Tel.: 020 7833 0022
Website: www.alcoholics-anonymous.org.uk
Provides information, and details of AA groups around the country.

**Befriending Network (Scotland) Ltd**
45 Queensferry Street Lane
Edinburgh EH2 4PF
Tel.: 0131 225 6156
Website: www.befriending.co.uk

**British Association for Counselling and Psychotherapy (BACP)**
BACP House
15 St John's Business Park
Lutterworth
Leics LE17 4HB
Tel.: 01455 550243
Website: www.bacp.co.uk
A membership organization and a registered charity that sets standards for therapeutic practice and provides information for therapists, clients of therapy and the general public. On request, they will send a list of your local qualified and accredited counsellors.

**Counsel and Care**
Twyman House
16 Bonny Street
London NW1 9PG
Tel.: 020 7241 8555
Website: www.counselandcare.org.uk
Provides help and information for older people, their families and carers.

**Cruse Bereavement Care**
PO Box 800
Richmond TW9 1RG
Tel.: 020 8939 9530
Helpline: 0844 477 9400 (staffed by volunteers, 9.30 a.m. to 5 p.m.,
Monday to Friday; extended to 7 p.m. on Mondays and Wednesdays)
Website: www.crusebereavementcare.org.uk
Provides help and support to those experiencing bereavement.

**Equality and Human Rights Commission**
3 More London
Riverside Tooley Street
London SE1 2RG
Tel.: 020 3117 0235
Helplines: 0845 604 6610 (England); 0845 604 5510 (Scotland); 0845 604
8810 (Wales)
Website: www.equalityhumanrights.com

**Foundation for the Study of Infant Deaths**
11 Belgrave Road
London SW1V 1RB
Tel.: 020 7802 3200 (general information and administration)
Helpline: 0808 802 6868
Website: www.fsid.org.uk
A national charity dedicated to helping those whose babies have died
suddenly, and to research into cot death. Publishes an e-newsletter. There
are offices around the country; details are available from the website.

**FRANK (National Drugs Helpline)**
Tel.: 0800 77 66 00 (free, confidential advice 24 hours a day, 365 days a year)
Website: www.talktofrank.com

**Mental Health Foundation**
9th Floor, Sea Containers House
20 Upper Ground
London SE1 9QB
Tel.: 020 7803 1100
Website: www.mentalhealth.org.uk
A mental-health charity committed to helping not only in situations of
mental ill health, but to help everyone lead mentally healthy lives. There
are also offices in Scotland and Wales.

**Mind**
15–19 Broadway
Stratford
London E15 4BQ
Tel.: 0300 123 3393 (Mind*info*Line)
Website: www.mind.org.uk
A mental-health charity that provides high-quality information and
advice to assist in taking control of one's own mental health. Details of
associations and Mind shops in your own locality are available from the
website, which is shared with Mind Cymru (see below).

**Mind Cymru**
3rd Floor, Quebec House
Castlebridge
5–19 Cowbridge Road East
Cardiff CF11 9AB
Tel.: 029 2039 5123
Website: As above

**Miscarriage Association**
C/o Clayton Hospital
Northgate
Wakefield WF1 3JS
Tel.: 01924 200 795 (administration)
Helpline: 01924 200 799 (free, Monday to Friday, 9 a.m. to 4 p.m.)
Website: www.miscarriageassociation.org.uk
Provides help and support for those who have experienced miscarriage.

**National Drugs Helpline – see FRANK**

**NHS Direct**
Tel.: 0845 46 47
Website: www.nhs.uk
For general advice on all aspects of health; the website includes pages on
stress.

**No Panic**
93 Brands Farm Way
Randley
Telford
Shropshire TF3 2JQ
Tel.: 0808 808 0545 (free helpline, every day, 10 a.m. to 10 p.m.)
Website: www.nopanic.org.uk
Provides information and support for panic attacks, phobias, obsessions.

**Rape Crisis**
Tel.: 0808 802 9999 (free helpline, noon to 2.30 p.m.; 7 p.m. to 9.30 p.m.)
Website: www.rapecrisis.org.uk
There is no central office, but there are centres around the UK. A local
telephone directory should provide details if you have no internet access.

**Samaritans**
Tel.: 08457 90 90 90 (free, 24-hour service)
Website: www.samaritans.org.uk
The leading organization that assists those in despair or contemplating
suicide.

**Scottish Association for Mental Health**
Brunswick House
51 Wilson Street
Glasgow G1 1UZ
Tel.: 0141 530 1000
Website: www.samh.org.uk

**SupportLine**
PO Box 2860
Romford
Essex RM7 1JA
Tel.: 01708 765222
Helpline: 01708 765200 (hours vary, ring for details)
Website: www.supportline.org.uk
SupportLine provides a confidential telephone helpline offering emotional
support to any individual on any issue, including bullying and loneliness.

**Victim Support**
Hallam House
56–60 Hallam Street
London W1W 6JL
Tel.: 0207 268 0200
Supportline: 0845 30 30 900
Website: www.victimsupport.org

**Women's Aid Federation**
PO Box 391
Bristol BS99 7WS
Tel.: 0808 2000 247 (freephone 24-hour service, run in conjunction with Refuge).
Website: www.womensaid.org.uk
The key national charity working for an end to domestic violence against women and children. There are also Federations in Scotland, Ireland (both Northern Ireland and the Republic) and Wales. In each part of the UK the particular Federation co-ordinates the network of local domestic-violence organizations, refuges and support services. Local telephone directories will give local details.

## Websites

**Staying positive**
BBC
http://news.bbc.co.uk/1/hi/programmes/happiness_formula/

European Network for Positive Psychology
www.enpp.eu

University of Pennsylvania
www.authentichappiness.sas.upenn.edu

**Stress**
Health and Safety Executive
www.hse.gov.uk/stress

International Stress Management Association UK
www.isma.org.uk

UK National Work-Stress Network
www.workstress.net

www.workhealth.org
An American site dealing with various aspects of work-related stress.